Changing Times
SERIES

PECKHAM
AND NUNHEAD
remembered

Numerous postcards still exist showing what Peckham was like in the early years of the twentieth century. Despite hardships, many former residents have happy memories of life in Peckham and Nunhead before the Second World War.

Changing Times
SERIES

PECKHAM
AND NUNHEAD
remembered

Compiled by
John D. Beasley

TEMPUS

First published 2000
Copyright © John D. Beasley, 2000

Tempus Publishing Limited
The Mill, Brimscombe Port,
Stroud, Gloucestershire, GL5 2QG

ISBN 0 7524 2051 8

Typesetting and origination by
Tempus Publishing Limited
Printed in Great Britain by
Midway Clark Printing, Wiltshire

Cover picture: *Queens Road in around 1904 showing Peckham Wesleyan church.*

Other books by John D. Beasley:

Building Together: The Story of Peckham Methodist Church
Peckham Methodist Church, Wood's Road, London SE15 2PX
Who Was Who in Peckham
Chener Books Ltd, 14 Lordship Lane, London SE22 8HN
The Bitter Cry Heard and Heeded:
The Story of the South London Mission of the Methodist Church 1889-1989
South London Mission, Central Hall, Bermondsey Street, London SE1 3UJ
Peckham and Nunhead Churches
South Riding Press, 6 Everthorpe Road, London SE15 4DA
Peckham Rye Park Centenary
South Riding Press
Transport in Peckham and Nunhead
South Riding Press
East Dulwich: An Illustrated Alphabetical Guide
South Riding Press
The Story of Peckham and Nunhead
Southwark Local Studies Library, 211 Borough High Street, London SE1 1JA
The *Imaged of England* Series: *Peckham and Nunhead*
Tempus Publishing, Brimscombe Port, Stroud, GL5 2QG

Contents

Lilian Tandy lived in Peckham for most of her life from the age of four until she died in 1999 aged ninety-eight. She watched the Tower Cinema being built from her classroom in Wood's Road School and was reprimanded for looking at German prisoners of war on Peckham Rye during the First World War. Mrs Lilian Burden, as she became, provided information on local history previously unrecorded. She was the oldest reader of The Peckham Society News.

On 4 June 1951 a No. 84 tram stops close to Nunhead Lane before proceeding to the terminus at Stuart Road. The former steam bus garage, opened in 1911, can be seen a short distance away.

Introduction

'In plucking the fruit of memory one runs the risk of spoiling its bloom', so wrote the Polish-born English novelist Joseph Conrad in 1924. Former Peckham and Nunhead residents, some of whose memories go back further than the twenties, have spoilt nothing by recording their memories for this book. In fact, they have shed a new light on the area.

As a Yorkshireman, who was brought up in Lincolnshire in the forties and fifties, I found that memories of my own childhood were triggered by some of the contributions to this book. My parents ran a hardware and ironmongery shop so I knew about hearthstone and blue bag. Caning in schools brought back painful memories! Monday was washday in Grimsby and Peckham. In our shop we sold dolly sticks and tubs. When I was being bathed in front of the coal fire in the living room, I told my sisters not to look. Many Peckham and Nunhead residents had no bathrooms so all the family used the same water in a zinc bath. Like many Peckham people, our family had an outside toilet. When I visited my grandma in Hull, pieces of the *Daily Mirror* were used as toilet paper.

As I was born in 1944, I do not remember the last war but some Peckham residents have vivid memories of both World Wars. One was reprimanded for looking at prisoners held in huts on Peckham Rye during the 1914-18 war. Another has written about people being killed when the King's Arms took a direct hit. Though there was much poverty, former residents have many happy childhood memories. Like many Peckham children, I too played hopscotch and 'he' in Grimsby. As we had a shop, we never left a key on the end of a piece of string fastened to the front letterbox but we did sometimes leave it under the mat in the outside toilet.

Trams ran in front of my bedroom window when I was a child, and I went to my junior school by tram when I had a spare penny (which wasn't often!). Trams were a familiar sight in Peckham. One 91-year-old former resident recalls seeing steam buses dropping hot ash in Rye Lane.

Peckham's main shopping street was, and still is, Rye Lane which used to be known as the Golden Mile. The former Jones and Higgins tower, erected by 1896, still dominates the junction of Peckham High Street and Rye Lane. It is a reminder of a bygone era when the well-known departmental store occupied the site where the Aylesham Centre is today. Peckham has not been the same since Jones and Higgins closed – as I have been told many times after giving slide shows on the history of the area.

Peckham and Nunhead have undergone countless changes in the twentieth century. Holdron's, another large departmental store, closed in 1949 after being taken over by John Lewis. Shops in Rye Lane today reflect changes that have occurred in the local population since the last war. Other places around Britain have changed dramatically too in the last hundred years so Peckham is far from unique in this respect.

Former residents remember horse-drawn transport, and recall one horse that was taken through the house to the back garden at the end of each working day! Milk can no longer be bought from the dairy which had its own cows in Lugard Road. Cattle are no longer taken to a slaughterhouse in Reedham Street. Children cannot drown in the canal. Few homes now have a piano and barrel organs are no longer seen in the streets. Lamplighters have not been employed for many years and the big workhouse, known as the Spike, has been converted into flats. The Peckham Pioneer Health Centre, which became world-famous, is also now being converted into flats. Today Peckham Pulse, Britain's first healthy living centre, stands close to the new Peckham Library. which has received a remarkable amount of positive national publicity.

During the twenty-eight years that I have been an adopted Peckhamite, I have seen many changes. The Odeon and Astoria have been demolished, the former Gaumont is no longer a bingo hall, Austin's has been replaced with houses, and many unsuitable council flats in north Peckham have already been demolished. Grass now grows where the lido used to be. Peckham Rye Park, which holds happy memories for many former residents, remains the most beautiful park in the London Borough of Southwark. A plaque records that The Peckham Society organised the Centenary Celebrations exactly one hundred years after the park was created where Homestall Farm had been in Victorian times. Since its inaugural meeting on 7 October 1975, The Peckham Society has campaigned to improve SE15 and to preserve all that is best in Peckham and Nunhead. This book will be

A No. 40 tram heads along Peckham High Street towards New Cross Gate while a No. 36 bus goes to Hither Green station. A Royal Arsenal Co-operative Society store is on the north side of this busy main road and the tower of Jones and Higgins' departmental store awaits restoration after being damaged during the Second World War.

officially launched at a special event at The Peckham Settlement on Saturday 7 October 2000 to mark the Silver Jubilee of The Peckham Society. This important amenity society, affiliated to the Civic Trust, will continue to co-operate with local residents who all have a vital role to play in making Peckham and Nunhead friendly and pleasant places in which to live and work. It is hoped that all present and future residents will also have happy and interesting memories of SE15.

Acknowledgements

This book has been written by people who have a wide variety of memories of that part of south-east London which, since 1917, has had the numbered postal district SE15. The pictures have come from various sources including some of the contributors of the memories. Among the people to whom I am grateful are Kathleen Adams, Derek Austin, Valerie Austin, John Barnes, Magna Bartosch, Margaret Berry, the late Reginald Bond, Agnes Boyle, Joan Brown, Lilian Buckley, Lilian Burden (who did not live long enough to see the book published), Norman Burrows, Ray Byfield, Margaret Chandler, Marina Clayton, Janet Cole, Eileen Conn, Vera Constable, Vera Conway, Joyce Cordwell, Doris Daniels, the late Cecil Edgell, Harold and Pam Elven, Ernie Fox (Queensland, Australia), Norma Francis, Irene Goodwin, Roger Hards, Barbara Kennedy, Stanley Kettel, Sam King, Simon Kogan, Norman Lenton, Peggy Lovett, Winifred MacKenzie, Leonard Moncrieff, Val Mucklow, Myrtle Newman, Valerie Newman, Peter Norman, Bill Payne, Joan Payne, Mrs V. Pearl, Leonard Phillips, Ted Pickett, Charles Preuveneers, Janet Rose, Reg Simmonds, Grace Smith-Grogan, Bob Smyth, Doreen Spence, Nellie Thornton, Pat Timlin, Walter Veale, Lesley Wakefield, Dorothy Walmsley and Tim Ward. Southwark Local Studies Library provided pictures of the Peckham Pioneer Health Centre and Free Form Arts Trust donated a slide of the Tower Cinema entrance. Gill Frost read the original typescript and made many helpful suggestions. I also appreciated her reading the proofs.

If readers know where pictures of Wilson's fair and Avondale Road Unitarian church can be found I shall be extremely grateful to be told as extensive research has failed to locate any. Similarly, I should be glad to have the opportunity to borrow other old photographs of Peckham and Nunhead which can then be copied for deposit in the excellent Southwark Local Studies Library.

Author's note: Most of the memories that follow were collected by the author in 1999 and early in 2000. A date is shown following the speaker's name, in most cases, when this was not the case.

CHAPTER 1

Homes

Acorn Buildings were demolished in the early 1960s to make way for the Acorn Estate. The spire of Peckham Methodist church can be seen in the background.

My Birthplace

I was born on 1 January 1938 in Acorn Buildings which were demolished in the 1960s to make way for the Acorn Estate. My grandfather, who was a tram driver, married my grandmother in 1893. I don't know when they moved into 'the Buildings' as they were called. When my parents married

in 1929 they took up residence in No. 28. Various relatives lived in nearby flats. I have many happy memories of my comfortable home although it seems primitive by today's standards. Our flat was on the first floor and was reached by a stone staircase which was washed every week by one of the tenants.

On entering the front door, which had a brass knocker and letterbox highly polished

Left: *Winifred Steel stands with her father on the roof of Acorn Buildings.* Right: *Winifred Steel sits with her dolls.*

by my mother, there was a small lobby. Opposite was the bedroom which I shared with my parents. I slept in a drop-sided cot until we moved in 1944 because there was not enough space for another bed.

To the left of the lobby was the 'front room' which looked on to the 'square'. The front room contained the best furniture and was seldom used but was dusted and polished every week. To the right of the lobby was our living room which contained a small black range, which was always alight, a grandfather clock, a deal table covered with a red, fringed cloth and two chairs with wooden arms. The window in the room did not let in much light as the next block of flats overshadowed us. At the end of the living room was the door into

a tiny kitchen which contained a stone sink and wooden draining board with shelves underneath covered by a curtain, a small one-burner gas cooker and a wooden 'Star' wash boiler. On the left of the kitchen was our 'lav', which was most unhygienic by today's standards.

Winifred MacKenzie (née Steel)

Crowded Houses

My grandmother and great-grandmother came to live in London at the turn of the last century. When they married, my grandparents rented a house at Chadwick

No. 13 Chadwick Road was rented for a few shillings a week. The railings were removed for the war effort.

Road, for a few shillings a week, from Andrews (now Andrews and Robertson). They shared the house with my great-grandmother until her death in 1913, by which time my mother had been born (in the same room in which she died in 1989). In 1936 my mother married her neighbour's lodger and they moved in with my grandparents. I find it hard to appreciate that our little terraced houses were homes to people with quite large families or who took in lodgers. Our house was larger than some of the others and we shared with another family who lived upstairs.

Norma Francis

Trees in Harder's Road

I was born above a shop in the High Street in 1913. When I was two we moved to 37 Harder's Road where I lived until 1975. I remember the large trees in Harder's Road. They were so large you could not get two arms to reach around the trunk. They were cut down when I was about twelve and I cried. Wealthy families lived in the large houses in Harder's Road. They went out using ponies and traps. There was a short tram line in Harder's Road where trams from the High Street turned round.

Lilian Buckley

Boys and Girls Lived Separately

The London County Council Peckham Children's Home in Stuart Road was called

Lilian Buckley lived at 37 Harder's Road which was demolished so that the Cossall Estate could be built in the 1970s.

The Newlands. There were six houses for the girls with twelve in each house. Ages ranged from three to sixteen years. The lady in charge of each house was called 'Mother' and the assistants, either one or two, were called 'Auntie', and it was run like a real family. Of course, there was discipline, but on the whole we were happy, with treats at Christmas. We went away for holidays. We went out to school, mainly to Ivydale Road, and were also free in our spare time to go out to play in the yard behind the house or in Peckham Rye Park and on Peckham Rye Common, or to walk around the district. The boys were housed separately in some houses across a field next to The Newlands. Brothers and sisters were able to meet regularly, and relatives were able to visit. Some of the older children were sent to other private houses in the district, taken over by the LCC. Two examples were houses in Crystal Palace Road and Friern Road, still with the same set up with a house mother, etc. and going out to various schools, depending on whether children had passed scholarships. The Newlands was still the headquarters. The Peckham Children's Home closed down in about 1935, and we were then sent to other Homes in Anerley and Norwood.

A former resident

Grandmothers Were Different

I was born at No.15 Brabourn Grove, Nunhead in June 1924. My father's family had lived in the Peckham and Camberwell area for many years. When my parents married they lived in Brabourn Grove with my paternal grandmother who occupied a flat on the second floor. She was to live there for twenty years, until her death when she was buried in Nunhead Cemetery.

My father's mother was a forbidding

Most residents at The Newlands attended Ivydale Road School.

Victorian widow who wore severe black all the time with a black poke bonnet. Her strict outlook on life showed quite clearly in her attitude towards her two grandchildren. In twenty years' living with my parents she never once agreed to look after them. She believed and said, 'You have the children and it is your responsibility to look after them'. My maternal grandmother was quite different. She was a plump jolly lady who loved her many grandchildren dearly and would do anything for them. Unfortunately she suffered with asthma and lived some way from us so we could only meet when the large family on my mother's side were able to get together during celebrations for Easter, Christmas, weddings and other similar festivities.

Harold Elven

Clothes Workshop at Home

I was the youngest of three children and our family lived in a barn of a flat in the High Street. It had a long staircase from street level, a large room just at the top of the stairs on the right, the kitchen next to it, a large square hall with another large room on the left-hand side, with a small room at the bottom of the staircase which led up to the attic rooms. In the middle side wall of the hall were a couple of steps to a wide corridor with a large room on the left, which was the sitting room. On the right was another large room, which was the workroom as my parents were mantle manufacturers. They made coats and dresses for someone in the City. I cannot remember how many people worked in that room but my mother used to cut out the coats. She used to design clothes. I remember seeing some of her

Walter and Daisy Elven were photographed with their sons, Jack and Harold, in their garden at 15 Brabourne Grove in 1930.

drawings. My father used to do the pressing with large heavy irons. I can remember seeing the steam coming from the seams, and him soaping, with a special type of soap, on parts of the coats like the collar and revers. The only form of heating at times in this room was a small oil stove which a kettle could be put on the top of to boil water. One day I had had a tooth extracted and wasn't feeling well so was lying down on the sofa in the sitting room. Suddenly there was a call of, 'Fire'. The oil stove had gone up in flame but fortunately no real damage was done.

There was a doss-house next to our home where a lot of men stayed for the night. At

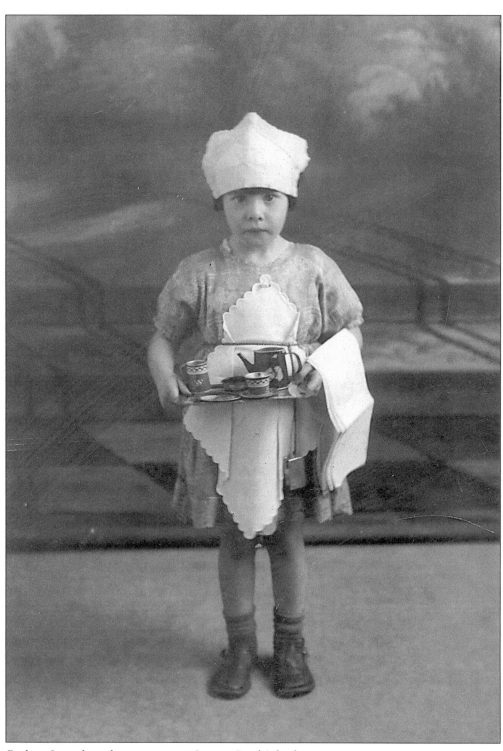

Barbara Jones dressed as a waitress at Sumner Road School.

times it smelt. I was always afraid to pass the front door.

Barbara Kennedy (née Jones)

Mushroom Picking

Our house was a terraced property, three up three down, close to Gloucester Road School; it was some sixty to seventy years old. Grandmother used to reminisce about the times when she used to go and gather mushrooms in the morning for breakfast in the fields now long since covered with housing.

Stanley Kettel

House Flooded

I've lived in Oxenford Street for forty-seven years and seen many changes since central heating was put in. Before the drains were improved, whenever there was a heavy storm our street was flooded. Water went in the front door and came out in the back garden where it was about three feet deep. Sewage came up from the drains. Firemen once pumped 400 gallons of water from our house.

Nellie Thornton

Homes Changed

What a difference fifty years have made to our living standards! We started with an outside toilet, cold water tap in the scullery and a copper to heat water. The latter was a built-in water container with a small open fire underneath and was used to heat water for washing clothes and baths (a tin bath in front of the fire). We had gas lighting and a gas stove, which replaced the kitchen range for cooking. I still own a mangle, the device for wringing water from the wet washing. I still think it was more effective than a spin dryer, although harder work. Sheets went through the wringer, or mangle, and needed minimal ironing. There was a larder to keep food as cool as possible with a mesh-covered box, called a meat safe, to keep any flies from fresh food. Not having a fridge was less of a problem than it would be today because shopping was a daily occurrence, and fresh food would be used up in two or three days. Milk was delivered daily but in the summer it still needed to be kept cool so my dad dug a brick-lined well in the garden. This had a double lid for insulation. It was very effective.

Also in the days before electricity, we had a radio (or wireless) that ran on accumulators. These were large, very heavy, wet-cell batteries which needed to be topped up, at the local shop, with acid. These were obviously quite hazardous, and most people replaced them with electric radios or transistorised radios with dry cell batteries as soon as it was possible. By the sixties many people had televisions and would invite not so fortunate neighbours in to watch special programmes.

Norma Francis

Tar-Covered Blocks for Fuel

In 1926 when Commercial Road (now Way) was being resurfaced, everyone was allowed to dig up the wooden blocks covered in tar. We used hammers and chisels. Then we put them in sacks and carried them home in prams and carts. They burnt well on the kitchen range but created a lot of soot so then we had to get the chimney sweep.

Nellie Thornton

Safe with Unlocked Doors

We all left our doors open and if mum was out working we could go into our friends' homes. We always felt safe.

Marina M. Clayton (née Morris)

Cocoa for First Time

One day I was playing in a friend's house and was given a cup of cocoa. This was the first time I had ever tasted it. It was lovely. I told my mother when I got home and eventually she bought a tin of Van Houten cocoa. That became our nightly drink.

Barbara Kennedy

Help with Housework

My mother had a disabled woman come in to do the heavy housework. As she had only one arm, it must have been hard for her to do some of the chores. As I look back, I realise that we were very poor but my mother managed to have a woman to help her but I expect it cost only a shilling or two and she may have been given a meal to make up for wages.

Barbara Kennedy

Pianos and Singing

At Christmas time there was more than one Father Christmas offering us a dip from his sack for ld or 2d. After Christmas dinner we went for a walk in the neighbourhood. Curtains were not drawn. Nearly everyone owned a piano and there was always a pianist with everyone singing. People wore party hats. Balloons were hung and decorations were often hand-made by children. There were Christmas crackers called bon-bons. The cheerful firelight glow completed the picture of a happy and stable family life for many people despite the poverty.

Grace Smith-Grogan

CHAPTER 2

Education

Children at Lyndhurst Grove Infants School dressed up in about 1929. The teacher on the left is Miss Butterworth who was just starting her career.

Played Truant

I started at Lyndhurst Grove infants in 1928. It was a dreary walk up and down the hill. We all came home at dinner time. The smell of privet flowers still reminds me of my trudge. I was indeed a tardy scholar. I hated school. My friend Gwyneth (who now lives in Wales) and I started together. We found school boring and played truant a few times. It had to stop when my dad told us our pictures were in the *Police Gazette* and our mothers might have to go to prison with Gwyneth's baby brother!

Kathleen Adams

Father Made Crown

At the age of six, in 1925, I was chosen to be Queen at the open day for parents at Ady's

Some pupils at Lyndhurst Grove Girls' School wore gymslips in about 1932. There were forty-three children in the class.

Road Infants School. The boy King wore a cardboard crown covered with gold paper. My father, a craftsman in the brass trade, decided to make a brass crown replica of Queen Victoria's. It was a beautiful crown and everyone gasped with amazement – except me. I wanted a cardboard one the same as the boy King's. I felt very embarrassed.

All the teachers and parents were enchanted by the little curly-haired girl with her beautiful headgear sitting on a small wooden table throne. Everyone was happy except me. The crown came in very handy to play with at home when we played charades or made up our own plays. We had an old trunk full of dressing up clothes. Alas the little crown disappeared when we were bombed out of our home during the Blitz. My father also made a splendid helmet, shield and trident, but not with brass, when I was chosen to be Britannia in a lovely pageant arranged by the 100th London

Company of the Girls' Life Brigade which used to meet at Rye Lane Baptist chapel.

Grace Smith-Grogan

Tea at Teacher's Home

I attended Bellenden Road School and after the end of term the first three in the results had their photograph taken. In addition we were invited to our teacher's home for tea, which to me was almost as good as being invited to Buckingham Palace.

Dorothy Walmsley

Clark's College

Clark's College at Peckham Rye was a commercial college which also had a junior school which my sister and I both attended. I went there in 1930 and I still have my term reports. The headmaster was Mr Underwood who had lost an arm in the Great War of 1914-18. The secretary was Miss Green and our first teacher in the first form was a wonderful lady whose name was Miss Shockley who taught us reading, writing and arithmetic. We had copy books for writing with thin strokes up and thick strokes down using pens and blotting paper. By the time I was seven I think I could write far better than I can now! It was such a happy place and I can remember how at Christmas we made paper chains and Christmas cards. We had a pillar box for the classrooms so that we sent our cards to our school friends. My mother walked us to school in the morning from our house at 28 Gowlett Road where I was born on 14 June 1925. She walked

down to collect us at lunchtime, gave us lunch, walked us back again and then collected us at 4 o'clock. Brookstone Court stands on the site of the school. I went on to Haberdashers' Aske's School at New Cross but I was never as happy there as I was at Clark's College.

Derek Austin

Punished with Canes

I was born in 1925 and Gloucester Road School provided my elementary education from the age of five to eleven. In the infants we were exposed to the kindly ways of the headmistress, Miss Malion, and another kindly lady called Miss Harmon. Classes were in the region of forty pupils and desks were the order of the day. When

Bellenden Road School pupils wore uniforms when Dorothy Walmsley attended it.

In 1930 Gloucester Road School had stepped classrooms.

the time came to go up to the senior school, life took on an altogether different aspect. The headmaster, a tall white-haired gentleman called Snelling, kept a bundle of canes in his study. His favourite torture was to despatch those who displeased him to get a cane and make sure it was number thirteen. On returning, the miscreant received three slashes across the upturned palm of each hand in front of an admiring mixed class. Another sadistic teacher was a gifted artist who also used his enormous hands to administer fearsome clouts around the ears and head.

Stanley Kettel

Prizes Presented

I attended Gloucester Road School where Mr William Margrie, who was known as the Sage of Peckham, gave out prizes to those who did good work or attended regularly. He was a very tall man who had a big moustache.

Nellie Thornton

Honor Oak School

I was born in Peckham in 1920 and spent the first twenty years of my life in Wellington Road (later re-named Belfort Road), a turning off St Mary's Road and close by the lovely St Mary's church, also a later victim of the Blitz. At the age of three I was enrolled in the Babies' Class at Waller Road School. We were living in an upstairs flat at the time, and the patter of my tiny feet over the linoleum disturbed the two maiden ladies living below. For the sake of peace I was sent to school early, but

I do not think this was a disadvantage because by the time I was five and ready for the main school I had become accustomed to school discipline and had a basic knowledge of the alphabet.

At the age of eleven I obtained a Junior County Scholarship which was considered quite an achievement. The next stage was to find a place in a Secondary or Grammar School. Application was made to Addey & Stanhope, and Aske's, Hatcham, but both were refused. I have a strong feeling this was because my father's occupation was 'coach painter – signwriter', and I was therefore the lowest of the low – a scholarship girl, applying for fee-paying schools.

My parents then turned to Honor Oak School, Homestall Road, which was a London County Council Secondary School and had just moved into brand new premises at the top of Peckham Rye (now known as Waverley School). This was a good move. It had all facilities, was set in lovely grounds, and had a go-ahead staff with modern ideas. The joy of our young lives was the midday break when we played a game known as 'jumping the stream'. A rivulet ran to Peckham Rye Park through the centre of our grounds. We would start from one end, jumping from bank to bank, until we reached the other end where it ran from near the golf course. There was always a girl who went to afternoon class with wet feet, having slipped in.

I always walked to school via Gibbon Road and Linden Grove, along by Nunhead Cemetery and then through Solomon's Passage and across Peckham Rye and through the Park. This is where my memories of Nunhead Cemetery come from. I consider that I had a good, all-round education at Honor Oak. I duly matriculated and obtained an Intermediate County Scholarship. I could have used this to go on to Training College but I considered my parents had made enough sacrifices to keep me at school after the usual leaving age of fourteen, so I used this second scholarship for commercial studies in the sixth form commercial section. After a year I obtained the requisite Royal Society of Arts Certificates in Shorthand, Typing and Elementary Book-keeping, and obtained a very junior position with a company of meat importers in Smithfield Market. It was then late 1937 and everything seemed set fair, but of course 1939 was upon us and the Blitz.

Joan Brown

Leo Street School

My second school was Leo Street Secondary Modern School for Boys. The headmaster, Mr Croft, at assembly each morning would lay down the law regarding the amount of litter (there wasn't any) which was totally unacceptable; also his hatred of chewing gum (which, according to him, Americans waded knee-deep in) and jeans (also American) which were totally taboo.

Ray Byfield

Central School Trips

Peckham Central School was in Peckham Road opposite Peckham House. The building had been vacated by Peckham

Secondary School when they moved into a new school at Honor Oak. The girls from the Central came into that building leaving the boys' central in Choumert Road. In 1934 I joined Peckham Central School. The approach was pleasant. From the pavement a path through a shrubbery led into the playground. An attractive lawn and rose walk to the left were strictly for the older pupils to enjoy. The classrooms were painted in pastel colours. I had known only dull brown and green. Every morning at assembly we would listen to classical music until it was time for a simple prayer, a hymn and school news. We had a lamp as a focus of the well-being of the school. At a yearly ceremony the lamp was presented to the winning house and their colour would be reflected in the lamp. On some Friday afternoons we would have a speaker. Some were very good (but one or two were embarrassingly awful!). I remember Lady Reading speaking about the League of Nations and General Smuts' nephew told us about life in South Africa. I was unable to go home at dinner time after we moved away so I had a school meal and at 6d a day they were jolly good value. A cook and her helper worked very hard to provide a tasty dinner and pudding. This service was provided by the school. Some girls brought sandwiches and we all sat at tables with gingham table cloths in the hall.

Two of my class mates were married into the Adams family. Marcelle Smith married my brother-in-law, and they live in Canada. Betty Hazell married my husband's cousin Fred Elvy. On open day parents would be delighted with the standards of the school. In our well-equipped cookery centre, under the watchful eye of Miss Graham, the cake making and decorating was wonderful. I enjoyed cookery classes and would make myself unpopular at home by telling my mum what she was doing wrong. We had enthusiastic teachers some young and some not so young. They did their best with a motley crew of fast growing up young women.

We were taken to museums and places of interest. A visit to St Katharine's Dock was fun. In the warehouses we saw things imported, from far afield, including cork and elephants tusks. In the bonded vaults the man in charge of the sherry casks offered us a taste from some of them. We all enjoyed that educational outing. Wherever we travelled in London we went on a London County Council tram. The LCC ran them as well as our school. A train ride to Southampton one day was quite memorable. We were shown over the *Berengaria*, a luxury liner. We were lost for words, such a lifestyle was unimaginable to us. The decorations in the bedrooms and the dining rooms were gorgeous and they even had a swimming pool on the ship. We had seen places like that in 'the pictures'. It was hard to take in that people actually lived like that. As the day wore on we, with hundreds of other kids, assembled in the newly built dry dock. Not for long was it a dry dock. The heavens opened and the rain came down in 'stair rods'. Everybody was soaked. Our teachers were tremendous. Once on the train we all undressed, including the teachers, who did their best to keep us warm and to dry some of our clothes on the way home.

Miss Ambler encouraged us to take an interest in many things in our last year. We were shown around our local Camberwell Town Hall, an afternoon was spent in County Hall having things explained to us and then we went to the Houses of

Boys and girls had separate classes in Sumner Road School in 1935.

Parliament. Miss Ambler was a very capable lady. I have a book about Lambeth written by her.

The school took pupils from a wide range of homes in South East London and very skilfully gave us self-respect and a pride in our school. The school motto seems a bit idealistic in these days:

Whatsoever things are just and pure, Whatsoever things are lovely, think on these things.

Kathleen Adams

Father's Horse and Cart

My grandmother used to tell me how much she hated Sumner Road School and was only good at needlework. One day she had to stand on the form for talking in the lesson – and from this high position she could see through the classroom window. Suddenly, she saw her father passing by with his horse and cart. Forgetting where she was, she yelled and waved to him.

Vera Conway

School Injuries

I went to Sumner Road School when I was three and for the first few days I cried for my sister who was up in the bigger school. When I was older, several friends and I used to see how many of the stairs, leading to the upper floor of the cookery centre, we could jump down to the ground. I know I did quite a number and one day hurt my ankle but wouldn't tell anybody and was back again the next day for more jumping. When my sister was eleven she went to Peckham

A glimpse of life in Sumner Road School in the 1920s.

Forty-five children were in this class in Sumner Road School in the 1920s.

Central School which was a little way further along the High Street. During the summer school holidays we sometimes went to another school also along the High Street as they had playgroups or something going on. They also had a grassy play area and one day I sat on a bee and got stung. I cried so much I had to be taken home.

Barbara Kennedy (née Jones)

Received Prize

In Wood's Road School the infants were on the ground floor, the boys on the first floor and the girls had to walk up to the second floor. Each section had its own headmaster or headmistress. When I was a pupil, Mr William Brenchley was the headmaster for the boys and Miss E.M. Schofield was the girls' headmistress. We

were scared of her. She was a very strict disciplinarian. When the *Titanic* was sunk, we had to write a composition on it. My teacher, Miss James, sent me out to ask the headmistress to read it. She said it was very good and gave me a book called *Hereward the Wake*.

Lilian Burden

Headmaster Became Mayor

Wood's Road School was only two minutes' walk from my home. In 1925, just before I was twelve, I transferred from there to Peckham Central School in Choumert Road where I stayed until 1929. One year was most memorable because our headmaster, Mr Herbert Shalders, was Mayor of Camberwell. He often wore his regalia and we learnt something about the history of Council work. I am proud that

Walter Finch stands outside Waverley School in August 1988 when he was the chair of governors. He was also chairman of the Institute of Medical Laboratory Technology. Finch Way commemorates him and the Origin of Names in Peckham and Nunhead was dedicated to him.

Walter Finch, after whom Finch Way was named, attended the same schools as myself. He was actively involved in Peckham Methodist church for over sixty years. He trained as a microbiologist and became Vice Principal of Paddington College.

Lilian Buckley

School Bells Rang

School bells summoned pupils in the morning and afternoon. Each had a different sound. Pupils had a satchel strapped to their back or carried an attache case weighed down with books. In the playground skipping ropes, peg tops and netballs were popular.

Grace Smith-Grogan

CHAPTER 3

Health and Hard Times

Women enjoyed the keep fit class on the roof of the Peckham Pioneer Health Centre in St Mary's Road.

Pioneer Health Centre

I was a child of the thirties and grew up in the area that was chosen for the famous Peckham Experiment, which took place from 1926 until 1950. From 1935 it was run as a family club in a specially designed three-storey building in St Mary's Road which became known as the Pioneer Health Centre. The building had ample space and facilities with visibility and access for the leisure of up to 1,000 neighbourhood families. Everyone could see what others were doing and the sight of action promoted action. The centrally situated swimming pool was always the stimulus to action. Life

A new Peckham Pioneer Health Centre was built on the site of these nineteenth-century houses in St Mary's Road.

for me at the Pioneer Health Centre – affectionately known as 'The Centre' by member-families – was to be a unique experience. It began when my parents joined the Centre shortly after it first opened. We were a family of four at the time. I was seven and my sister Norma was just a few weeks old. On the first occasion that I entered the building everywhere appeared so vast – so many windows, so much light, and the swimming pool surrounded by glass was an awesome sight to a mere seven-year-old who had never seen a swimming pool before. For us children there were many activities, with a freedom of choice. What began as a novelty became a way of life so we were never bored. I went from one activity to another – in the process

learning to skate and to ride a bike. I can remember watching children in the gym, swinging from the ropes and jumping onto the apparatus with ease and confidence and I longed to be able to do the same. But I was to discover I was nervous of heights and not at all happy to climb the wall bars or the large 'window frame' structure that extended along one wall and reached almost to the ceiling.

I kept to floor level using the balancing forms. The gym provided a spontaneous activity – 'free play' it was called with no do's and don'ts. I was happiest on the forecourt and I must have spent hours roller skating and riding a bike. The cross-section of families who joined the Centre meant that children, regardless of their background, became good social mixers. We became confident and at ease mixing with adults. I was a shy child before joining the Centre, having had little contact with children outside school, so it was a totally new experience to be able to mix with a lot of children in a social environment. I had a happy childhood, but it was the Centre that gave me self-confidence and the happiest childhood memories.

My parents were active members too and enjoyed badminton and ballroom dancing. My father took up snooker and table tennis. In the second phase (1946-1950) he joined the drama group and played the piano for dancing. He composed a waltz, which he called 'The Centre Waltz' and would play it on Saturday nights. None of these activities

would have been part of their lives without the Centre.

They showed no interest in swimming, which meant as a family we didn't use the pool, so I had to learn to swim by using the learners' pool. Once I could swim a length I progressed to the main pool. However, the joy of this achievement didn't last very long when I realised I didn't have the same confidence when in a much bigger pool, coupled with the fact that I was prone to ear infections. I didn't use the pool with the frequency of most children.

The centrepiece of health care at the Centre was the annual health overhaul at which every member's health was reviewed in terms of their biological, nutritional and social development. My parents were very

Girls gathering lupins in the grounds of the Peckham Pioneer Health Centre in 1937.

Family consultations were a principal feature of the Pioneer Health Centre.

grateful for these overhauls. I remember asking my mother what was going to happen and she explained that we were human guinea pigs for the doctors because they wanted to find out how healthy we were. I remember being greatly amused at this and went round telling aunts and uncles that I was a 'human guinea pig'. The family overhaul for me was an experience that I have never forgotten. I remember the sessions in the laboratory. The staff were always so friendly while measuring weight and height, testing eyesight, taking blood samples and explaining what they were going to do. At one particular overhaul with Dr Pearse, I had to walk across the floor of her consulting room and she praised my nice straight back and good feet. Dr Pearse always encouraged children to go barefoot whenever possible to let the feet expand freely. She explained the value of children

walking more in their bare feet to aid development of the bony structure of the feet – a principle adopted for my own children. It was discovered that I was anaemic and suffering from rheumatism. Dr Pearse arranged for me to have tests at the Royal Free Hospital. The school doctor had told my mother that I was suffering 'growing pains'. From a rather sickly child I developed into a more healthy one, with a good measure of self-confidence.

I remember that I would go to the Centre straight from school but before I went off to join my peers I would always find my mother in the cafeteria to let her know I was there. I sometimes liked to visit the nursery to see my sister Norma who would be there having her tea. A mother could leave her young baby or toddler in the nursery while she enjoyed some recreation elsewhere in the building. Afternoons of freedom at the

Centre for mothers of pre-school children completely changed their way of life. Many were deprived of any sort of social life before joining. Children were free to come and go on their own to the Centre. In the 1930s and 40s parents did not become anxious for their children's safety as would be the case today. There was very little traffic on the roads which meant that it was safer for us to get from school or from home. The Centre had to close at the outbreak of the Second World War and it didn't re-open until 1946. My parents re-joined, by which time their family had increased to three daughters. My sisters Norma and Veronica aged eleven and seven took an active part in the second phase with exuberance, enjoying all the facilities in the same way I had years before.

By this time I was eighteen and life at the Centre took on a new dimension. I joined the badminton club and by 1947 social evenings were frequently organised. A dance band was formed and on Saturday evenings there was always a dance, which would be attended by a mixture of teenage boys and girls and married couples. Around this time a Central Office of Information film was made on behalf of the Foreign Office for distribution overseas featuring the Peckham Experiment. The preparation and shooting of this film took several months. All the people taking part were member families and included many children and teenagers for crowd scenes. I remember that due to the film being made in June all the many night scenes had to be shot after midnight. But we didn't mind giving up our leisure. In fact, I remember I enjoyed watching the process of filming. It is documented that the producers frequently remarked upon the spontaneous and tireless way in which the ordinary and hardworking people gave up their leisure – their gift of

time, energy and enthusiasm was a very considerable one in order to present a permanent record of Centre life. That film was called *The Centre* and made a powerful impression. It inspired and illustrated the unique experience in living which the Centre member families had the privilege to enjoy. The first public showing took place in July 1948 at the Odeon Cinema in Peckham. After the performance, HM Queen Mary graciously consented to visit the Centre. The Prime Minister and many other distinguished guests were also present.

A young man came into my life in 1947 who was to become my future husband. Harold, better known by his nickname of Adge, was born in Nunhead and like me was a Centre member. With a mutual interest in ballroom dancing and badminton, our relationship developed. We became yet another couple to find romance through Centre membership. Adge was a member of the swimming club and spent a lot of time swimming and diving. He encouraged me with my swimming and taught me to dive. It was tough for me because I was not a confident swimmer – it was a case of 'what one does for love!'

We became engaged in 1949 and started to make plans for our wedding. We were looking forward to becoming a 'Centre family'. We planned to have children and to bring them up in the Centre environment. Sadly the Centre closed three weeks before our wedding in March 1950. The Peckham Experiment had come to an end. The closing was a tragedy and I felt robbed of something I had taken for granted. It had never occurred to me that it would not be part of my life once I was married. The Centre touched me in a special way. The experience enriched my life, and taught me how to live, and the importance of the unity of the family, the

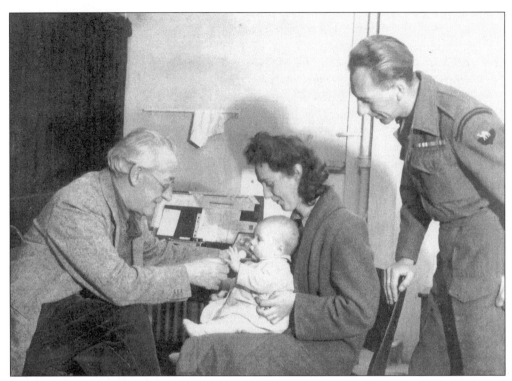

Dr George Scott Williamson, co-founder of the Peckham Pioneer Health Centre, undertaking a family consultation.

upbringing of my children, nutrition and self-awareness of a healthy body. Interest was aroused by the Peckham Experiment both at home and abroad and during the last fifteen months before it ended in 1950 – through lack of funds – no fewer than 12,000 visitors were received at the Pioneer Health Centre. Peckham can be proud that the world famous experiment into health promotion has become part of its heritage.

Pam Elven

Persuaded Parents

We watched with interest the building of the Pioneer Health Centre but soon got used to it. Once it was up and running I was invited by friends who were family members to go as a visitor. I could watch but could not participate in any way in the fascinating activities as only members were allowed to take part. I watched my friends play badminton, go to the gym and take part in unsupervised fun on the ropes, wall bars, vaulting and jumping equipment. All such equipment was normal in any gym but at the Centre was used in any fashion young minds could invent. I was fascinated by the whole concept and tried to get my parents to join but when they learned that they would have to have a medical overhaul on joining and an annual check-up the answer was a big, 'No!' To say that I was disappointed would be an understatement and I believe my parents knew this. However, I persevered and kept nagging away especially as I had several more wistful visits to the Centre, as I had learned to call it. Eventually after about six months I managed to get them to have a look, which they did one Saturday evening and they were so impressed after being shown around they consented to join, mainly for my sake I believe. From then on my life was the Centre. I took everything in my stride. I learned to play badminton, I played billiards and snooker for the first time and also table tennis. I learned ballroom dancing and the swimming pool, with its diving boards, was my joy. I very quickly became competent, as I swam and dived every night of the week.

My parents came to appreciate the Centre as well. My mother would go in the afternoon and soon made friends. To my utter astonishment she learned to swim when she saw others of her age and size in the pool. My father did not take part in any of the activities but enjoyed the atmosphere on Saturday evenings. His long hours of work prevented him from doing much more. The medical overhauls so much dreaded by them both, bore fruit. My mother had some internal disorder put right and my father had advice about his heart condition which I firmly believe to this day prolonged his life for many years,

After serving in the Royal Navy, I returned to Centre life once more – this time as an adult. I had a great interest in the work of this organisation. When I was asked by the director, Dr Scott Williamson, to work part-time in the evenings I was

As part of the routine examinations at the Pioneer Health Centre, all infants were seen weekly until taking solid food. Later they were seen fortnightly until they could walk.

Snooker competitions were enjoyed by the men who belonged to the Pioneer Health Centre.

delighted and readily complied and spent several years working with the children and, of course, adults if and when the children went home. It was at this time, I met the girl who was to be my wife. We married in 1950, the year that the Pioneer Health Centre closed. This was to be a black time in our lives. We had hoped to continue as members, and in due course to be a family of the Centre. Alas this was not to be. It is almost fifty years since the Centre closed but the memory lives as strongly as ever. My wife and I have tried to live our lives based on 'Principles of Peckham' and brought up our children in this vein. We have been very conscious of our health and the food we eat. We believe all this has served us well.

Harold Elven

Attended Centre

My family joined the Peckham Pioneer Health Centre not very long after it opened the new building in St Mary's Road in 1935. It was basically an experiment to discover and promote the growth of positive health but it also had excellent recreational facilities. Only families could join; individuals within a family could not join on their own. Every new member underwent an exhaustive medical examination which was at least as thorough as the medical examination I had before the Royal Air Force accepted me as an aircrew trainee in the Second World War. The difference was that whereas the latter was to see whether the volunteer's fitness was up to a prescribed level, the doctors at the Pioneer Health

Centre used the results of the examination to tell members not just what was wrong with them but what was right with them as well. At all times, not only when joining, members could obtain medical advice from the doctors. The recreational facilities included a swimming pool, a gymnasium and a theatre. All manner of pursuits could be followed, including billiards, snooker, table tennis and fencing, with instruction freely available to the uninitiated. The doctors who devised and ran the Health Centre, Dr Scott Williamson and Dr Innes Pearse, chose Peckham for their experiment because of the varying social structure found in the district. Family incomes in Peckham during the 1930s were said to be anything between £100 and £2,000 per annum and since the Health Centre attracted members from right across this band of income, there was a mix of social classes which would not otherwise have occurred. For example, I attended a secondary school in Deptford but became very friendly with a boy from Dulwich College whom I first met when playing cricket in the Health Centre grounds. I made many other friendships and certainly spent very many happy times at the Centre before the war. In 1948 Paul Rotha produced a film about the Health Centre. There was a story running through the film about a family joining the Health Centre and all the parts in it were played by Health Centre members. The lady who played the female lead was at school with me and is still a close friend. Due to financial difficulties the Health Centre closed in 1950 but in 1986 there was a very successful reunion of members there. I went to this and met many of the friends I had

Badminton was one of the games played in the Pioneer Health Centre. Here is the 1947/8 Badminton Club 'A' Team.

made nearly fifty years before. A company called Pioneer Health Centre Limited survived and in 1993 arranged for another film to be made about the Health Centre. It was called *A Pool of Information* and recalled the nature of the Centre and its aims. Several former members, including myself, were interviewed in the film.

Norman Lenton

Poverty in the Streets

Kerbstone men sold live baby chicks, yellow and fluffy, for 6d each. They were placed in a paper bag and carried away. Men who were blind, deaf or disabled in other ways, sold matches in shop doorways. Some openly begged in the street though it was against the law. Old soldiers, with arms and legs missing, struggled on crutches along the main road to the banging of a single drum. They were disabled by war and now jobless. Long queues of men – thin, pale and wearing flat caps – lined up outside the Labour Exchange. Little children stood outside pubs or sat on the steps often shivering with the cold much to my own parents' disapproval,

Grace Smith-Grogan

Smallpox Epidemic

In 1930 there was a smallpox epidemic; my brother and I caught the disease. I had just started working at the Quantock Laundry in Choumert Grove when two men in white coats came from the Town Hall and took me home. All the rooms in our house had to be

Two men in white coats went to the Quantock Laundry to take Nellie Thornton home. Here the staff are seen in 1935.

fumigated and we had to go to the Cleansing Station where our clothes and bedclothes were baked.

Nellie Thornton

Railway Allotments

We lived in Crewys Road which backed on to the railway and men had allotments on the bank. One kind gentleman would come down to our garden with lots of rhubarb and vegetables but did not want any payment. I think nearly everyone had chickens and rabbits in their garden. I doubt whether it would be allowed today.

Myrtle Newman

Monday was Washday

There was quite a sight to behold on Saturday mornings when housewives knelt on their kneeling mats and scrubbed their front door steps and forecourt. Soda was added to a pail of water to soften it. Hard yellow soap and scrubbing brushes were used. Very few women wore rubber gloves so hands were left red and sore. Doorsteps were finished with whitening stone called hearthstone. Entrances to houses were pristine white until the family had run up and down them a few times leaving dirty foot marks. Sometimes char women knocked offering to clean the steps for 6d. The shining windows had nicely starched lace curtains. We were never allowed to touch the curtains once they had been hung. My mother would fix the venetian blinds which were made from thin strips of

Grace Smith-Grogan seen here in 1942, aged 23, in her garden at 82 Ondine Road a year after getting married.

wood. They had to be dusted regularly and taken down at spring-cleaning time and washed. Family washing took place on a Monday morning. This was a ritual in our house. My mother would rise early to grate the soap. Yellow soap was rubbed on the cheese grater and then put with the dirty clothes which needed boiling in the large brick-built copper with a coal fire beneath. Some dirty clothes were scrubbed by hand on a washing board and then whitened with a blue bag. Wet clothes were put through a mangle, with large wooden rollers, after being washed. Children loved to turn the enormous handle. After the water had been squeezed out, the clothes were dried in the garden. Then they were put through the dry mangle. My sister, who had a fine thick mop of hair tied into a single plait almost down to her waist, had to suffer the indignity of her hair being rolled through the mangle every time it was washed. It dried beautifully. The plait was finished off by having the flat iron smoothed over it. The old-fashioned copper was later replaced by a gas boiler, then an electric boiler and finally an electric washing machine. Launderettes started to appear and they signalled the end of the old-fashioned washday as we knew it.

Grace Smith-Grogan

Biscuits Too Expensive

In the High Street, next to the dosshouse, was Brown's the bakers. Most days I went there for bread or something. I loved to look into the glass-lidded tins of biscuits. The nicest ones were the Punch and Judy biscuits but of course they were too expensive for us. We always had hot cross buns delivered on Good Friday morning. They were still hot and were great! My sister sometimes went to a grocer's shop near Jones and Higgins for a jar of marmalade or jam which cost 6½d for a 2lb jar. Once she dropped a jar and got told off.

Barbara Kennedy

Poor But Happy

In the 1920s Dr McKay had his surgery in Choumert Road. Sometimes he came to our home on his bicycle. My brother Bill had TB so my two sisters and I had to go for regular check-ups by Dr Brand at his surgery near St Giles' Hospital. I have happy memories of Peckham despite the poverty. Who cared that we had to put cardboard in our shoes or I had to wear my sister's out-grown coats, dresses and other clothes? We had different seasons for skipping, conker bashing, spinning tops with home-made whips and other pastimes. We saw silent movies at the cinema on Saturday mornings and attended Sunday school the next day in the old Gospel Hall. We lived only in our own world.

Marina Clayton

Outside Toilets

My memories and reflections of Peckham and Nunhead go back over fifty years when I returned to Britain from Jamaica on the SS *Empire Windrush* in 1948. My brother and I bought a house at 13 Castlemain Road, where part of the Gloucester Grove Estate was later built. It was a terraced house with lovely bay windows but the toilet was outside. At that time there were more horses and carts in Southampton Way than cars. There were even pigs in some front gardens. Donkeys, chickens and ducks were kept in large open spaces. Cyclists like myself found the ducks a nuisance because they were slow in getting out of the way of riders. A family member of mine bought a house in Somerton Road. When we were examining the back garden we discovered a well concealed by a concrete covering.

Sam King

The Slump

As the 1920s went into the 1930s the slump came and the mantle trade became very slack so we moved to the other end of Rye Lane to Rye Hill Park. We lived in a large house on the top of the hill. We lived opposite the water works. We had four rooms at the top of the house. There were two attic bedrooms. My sister and I had one room and it was so damp that we had fungus growing out of the walls. My parents and brother slept in the other bedroom. Downstairs there were two rooms. One was very large. My mother did the cooking in there. It was our living room. We ate in it and it was also a workroom. The other room was used for customers when they came.

Barbara Kennedy

Poor Childhood in Nunhead

I have an early recollection of being taken to school by my mother at the age of four in 1912. The school was in Consort Road. The teacher was Miss Price who kept control of the infants' class either by scolding us or giving us a boiled sweet to keep us quiet. We lived in Kirkwood Road and although we were poor I enjoyed a pleasant childhood. My father worked as an upholsterer. This work was seasonable so he was busy for three months before Christmas and then he had to seek other work to keep my mother, me and my two brothers. When snow covered the ground my father obtained temporary work removing it for Camberwell Council. Every child in Nunhead attended Sunday School – not that any of us were religious. The incentive was that in the summer at the end of the service we received a bunch of

Sam King was Southwark's first black Mayor. He is seen here in 1983.

primroses that we would proudly take home to give our mother who would reward us with a penny that was soon spent in buying treacle toffee. In the winter our reward after the service was two comics. For amusements in the summer we would gather conkers which we pickled in vinegar, to make them harder, while Mum was not looking. Another amusement was to tie the door knobs of two adjacent doors. We then banged hard on both doors and then, at a distance, watched the two householders trying to open the doors.

A treat was to be taken to the bandstand on Peckham Rye to listen to a regimental band playing classical music but this did not interest me much so I would wander away to see boys flying kites. At an early age I could see the class distinction as wealthy families headed by the master of the house, dressed in a frock coat and top hat, was followed by his wife (dressed in a sequin covered gown) and then followed by their children who were ushered to the front seats in front of the bandstand. When the First World War came, none of us was evacuated. My father was in the army in France. We still attended school and in the event of an air raid we would crouch under our desks. Very little damage was caused in Nunhead but I remember being taken by my mother to see the damage in Calmington Road where ten people died.

Our next door neighbours were the Smith family. The father was in a reserved occupation making guns. The family shared their meagre rations with us. People who lived in Kirkwood Road were very kind to us and in return we would run errands for the elderly folk who would reward us with a penny which we spent on a comic. After reading it, we swapped it for another.

Crime as we now experience it never occurred. Occasionally the milk would disappear but the majority of people were law-abiding even though they were on the brink of poverty. As lads we found our own amusements either walking to Greenwich Park or riding on the Woolwich Ferry imagining we were with Columbus to find the New World. Without the aid of calculators or computers, we left school competent in writing and reading. My first job was as an office boy to a poverty-stricken lawyer who could not find sufficient money to pay my weekly wage of ten shillings after six weeks. Lawyers in Camberwell had very few clients before the introduction of free legal aid.

Simon Kogan

Coalman's Horse and Cart

From an early age my sister Sylvia and I lived with our parents at 212 East Surrey Grove. It was a long road; our section was from Commercial Way to Camden Avenue and Peckham High Street. The Camden Arms pub graced the top of the road and we were well served by shops on every corner – Compton's the newsagents and confectioners, where we spent our penny pocket money, a general grocery shop, a post office and off-licence and a wonderful baker who baked on the premises. There was also an engineering company, The Expedite. The local scout hall and imposing scout master's house were features in the street. Major Lisle Watson lived there and every Remembrance Sunday a service was held outside his home. Although we were poor by today's standards, everyone took a great pride in their tiny front gardens – and net curtains. The street was regularly cleaned by a water cart.

Our house was a two up and two down terraced property with an outside toilet and no electricity – gas was the only form of heating and lighting. We had a large back garden where Mum and Dad grew vegetables and flowers. They also kept rabbits and chickens there and stored wood as fuel for the winter. The winters seemed dreadful and were made worse by pea soup fogs. Dad kept our sitting room fire going day and night for weeks by various means. It was a great comfort to sit around it in the evening with cups of cocoa and listen to the wireless or play cards.

We had a wonderful coalman, who came with a horse and cart when I was a child, and he never let us down. If our parents were at work when he called, he would deliver by letting himself into the house using a key on the string which was inside the letterbox attached to the lock, and leave the bill on the light switch saying, 'Pay next week'.

All the children loved the horse and fed him with carrots and sugar lumps. We thought he was so clever. When the horse saw the coalman leave a front door with his empty sack, he would walk to the next house without a command. In 1963, when the snow was deep, the coalman was unable to get down the street with a lorry, which had replaced the horse and cart. Knowing my father was very ill he carried the heavy sacks on his back from Commercial Way. I think his name was Mr Elliott.

Peggy Lovett

Crammed into Ophir Terrace

When I was six years old in 1944, I moved with my parents from Acorn Buildings to a small terraced house in Ophir Terrace which was a cul-de-sac off Bellenden Road. The move was accomplished by my father wheeling a barrow rented from the greengrocer's in Meeting House Lane. The house was small with two rooms and a scullery downstairs, two bedrooms upstairs and a small garden with outside lavatory. There was no bathroom. I was thrilled to have my own bedroom which my father painted green – my favourite colour. Second-hand furniture was bought for me – an old dressing table with a rather spotty mirror and many intriguing little drawers and a small wooden chair. In the kitchen-cum-scullery we had a copper in one corner which my father removed because my mother had a Star wash tub. This tub was wooden and had a long handle on the top, which had to be pushed back and forth to make the wooden dolly inside the tub rotate. We also had a small range and a one-burner gas cooker. How my mother managed to produce meals for six or more people at Christmas time, with such primitive equipment, still amazes me. The range was wonderful. Polished several times a week, it glowed and never seemed to go out. It gave light and heat to the room. We cooked on it and sat round it in the evenings, sometimes making toast on a long toasting fork or on special occasions cooking chestnuts.

We had a deep white sink in another corner and this is where we washed up and washed ourselves. Once a week the tin bath was brought in from the yard and we all had a bath – me first, my mother next and my poor father last – in the same water. Clean clothes were aired in front of the coal fire on a clothes horse. The room at the front of our house had our best furniture with a piano, which my mother sometimes played. The 'back room' had a table and chairs but these two rooms were rarely used as coal fires would have had to be lit to warm them. When I was older and my parents were more affluent, we used our front room and my father rented a television. My own children found it hard to understand when I told them about my childhood and how in winter we would put on a coat to go out to the lavatory. Old coats were hung on the back door for this purpose and a hurricane lamp or torch was put handy to light the way in the dark. Until after the Second World War our house was lit by gas light. It was my task to go to the small shops in Bellenden Road to buy the gas mantles. This was a very demanding task as they were so fragile but I actually managed to get them home intact.

There were lots of children living in Ophir Terrace and we would all go out to play together in the evenings. We played skipping, touch, ball in a stocking, handstands and hide-and-seek but the road cleared at 6.45 when all rushed inside to hear *Dick Barton (Special Agent)* on the radio.

Many of our neighbours would bring their kitchen chairs out into the street and sit and chat to each other on summer evenings. My father disliked this practice because he was a shy reserved man and was embarrassed to have to pass everybody on his way home. He called it 'running the gauntlet'. The houses had small front areas mostly without fences or gates. My father built a fence and gate for our house. While he worked he was serenaded by one of our elderly neighbours singing *Don't Fence Me In* (a popular song at the time). Into this small enclosure he put tubs and plants. With the window boxes, he made our house look quite attractive – so much so that one of our neighbours posed her daughter's wedding photographs in front of our house.

I was an only child but many of our neighbours had families of eight and nine children which meant that the downstairs front room was used as a bedroom as well as the two rooms upstairs. These families fought a continuing battle to keep clean and well dressed. My mother would often pass on my outgrown clothes to them and give the odd cup of sugar or flour and refuse payment. She was always full of praise for the way they coped with such large families.

Our main shopping centre was Rye Lane. Jones and Higgins was my favourite shop (not that we could afford to buy much there). At Christmas it had a beautiful toy department. The dolls, toys, books and games made it seem like Wonderland to me. One year when I was in my teens my mother bought a white Christmas crib in the china department. It cost £1 4s 0d and was, for my mother, a really extravagant purchase. I still have it today and it is much admired by my children and grandchildren.

I left 'The Terrace' as a bride in 1959 and the next year my, by then widowed, mother died. Later in the 60s the houses were demolished. I have many happy memories of my childhood in Peckham and remember with affection many of our neighbours and their children.

Winifred MacKenzie

Clothes Washed by Hand

Our house backed on to the railway line which ran from Nunhead station and I learned not to hear the trains passing which made most of the windows in the house rattle. Looking back I realise that the house was quite basic: no bathroom and an outside lavatory. We had a scullery with a built-in stone copper which my father stoked up every Monday – washday – which was always a busy day for my mother. Every item of clothing was washed by hand, using a ridged washing board and a bar of hard soap. All the whites including sheets and pillowslips were put in the copper for boiling, with a final rinse using Reckitt's Blue. The mangle we had was a monster in cast iron with big wooden rollers and it was my job, when I came home from school, to turn the handle while Mum fed in the wet washing to wring the water out and in some cases to press. Ironing was done using a solid heavy cast-iron flat iron which would be heated first on a gas ring. Some time later Mum became the proud owner of a gas iron. My father also stoked the boiler for Friday night baths which we had in a zinc bungalow bath. This, when not in use, was hung up on an outside wall.

Harold Elven

Kind Dr Tilbury

I was born in New Cross in 1923 and apart from service with the Royal Air Force in the Second World War, I lived there for twenty-eight years. Our family home was first in Musgrove Road and then from 1929, in Erlanger Road. Both roads are on the west side of New Cross and from Erlanger Road it was less than a quarter of a mile from where the New Cross SE14 postal district changes to Peckham SE15. As a result I had associations with Peckham from a very early age. My earliest visit to Peckham was to the surgery of our family doctor. It was in a large house between Pomeroy Street and York Grove and the doctor's surname was Tilbury. I recall him as an absolute gentleman who was always impeccably dressed in a black coat and vest and striped trousers. What I especially remember was his kindness. An example was when I was in the Brook Isolation Hospital in Shooters Hill Road in 1933, suffering from scarlet fever and my mother expressed concern to him about the time it was taking for me to recover. We were certainly not private patients, nor in any other way privileged, but the next day he drove to the hospital to see me and then reported back to my mother that all was well.

Generally, I much enjoyed going to Rye Lane. However, there was one circumstance in which going there filled me with dread. It was when we turned into Hanover Park to attend the LCC School Dental Clinic. I can still feel the almost excruciating pain caused by the treadle-operated drills the dentists used when filling teeth.

Norman Lenton

Sinister Peckham House

From 1925 until 1937 I lived in Bushey Hill Road SE5 – not strictly Peckham, but our lives were lived in Peckham. It was a long walk along Peckham Road to Rye Lane to do our shopping but never dull with lots of people and things to see. I can remember quite vividly the pictures that a pavement artist drew outside the then Peckham House. They were of the R101 disaster. Three pictures, the launch, flying aloft and the twisted remains, in wonderful detail. What a way to earn a few coppers! I hope that he became rich and famous. This was about seventy years ago. Peckham House, with its high walls and large wooden gates, was a strange place with a sinister feel about it. Occasionally a car or a coach with horses would go through the gates which were opened by men in livery. It frustrated me as I always tried to get a peep, but never ever saw the house. It was a mental home.

Kathleen Adams (née Roche)

CHAPTER 4

Transport

A No. 56 tram waits adjacent to Elland Road before proceeding to the Embankment on 2 June 1951.

Found a Gun

In 1963 my brother Harry Brooks, who was a cleaner at the London Transport garage in Bellenden Road, found a loaded .38 revolver and five boxes of ammunition under a rear seat in a bus. The gun was taken to Scotland Yard for examination.

Nellie Thornton

Tar Blocks Caused Fire

I loved the trams. My favourite seat was by the door with the amber coloured glass window, which turned everything yellow as you looked through it. When the tram era ended in 1952, the tramlines were removed together with the tar blocks in the roads

Harry Brooks (right) once found a loaded gun on a bus.

which were sold for fuel. These were cheaper fuel than coal but not as reliable.

When I was coming home from school one day I was greeted by fire engines called to deal with a chimney fire caused by the tar blocks. I thought it was exciting. My grandmother was making tea for the firemen, and my mum was only worried about what my dad would say when he came home from work.

Norma Francis

Saw Hay Bales

At one time granddad and grandma lived in Leyton Square. They moved from there to Melon Road at the back of the Tilling's depot. When I was taken by my mum to visit them, I used to sit at the window looking at the bales of hay going up on a conveyor belt for the many horses in the stables there. At the end of Melon Road was a blacksmith. I have seen him more than once at his forge, banging horseshoes into shape and then fitting them on.

Cecil Edgell

Cars Were Rare

There were few cars in the 1920s and buses did not travel up the east side of the Rye, but there were chocolate coloured tramcars which came up there and finished at Cheltenham Road.

Charles J.A. Preuveneers

A No. 56 tram waits at Peckham Rye terminus in October 1951.

Fire Engine Crash

In 1948 a fire engine, while answering a call, crashed through Cullen's shop window at the top of Rye Lane opposite The Triangle. I had just passed it with my baby in a pram.

Nellie Thornton

Canal Frozen

In winter the canal was frozen at Boathouse Walk and it was lovely to go and skate on it. There was no fear of the ice breaking as it was too thick. In the summer we watched all the rats swimming in the canal. Men used to collect the wood that had fallen off barges. It was used to make various things.

Nellie Thornton

Wet Legs

On open-topped buses, passengers used umbrellas and the storm covers which were unrolled from the seat in front. Little dents in the covers over your knees filled with water which would shower your legs when you got up as the cover was rolled up again. The stairs to the upper deck were positioned out in the open. They were very curved and precarious to climb.

Grace Smith-Grogan

Noises in the Night

I can remember the night-time noises very clearly. The goods trains, late trains and passenger trains and the different sounds of steam trains and the new electric trains. If the wind was in the right direction I could hear the ships' hooters from the docks.

Norma Francis

Horses and Carts

Milk was delivered by horse-drawn carts. The milkman placed a measuring jug into a churn and poured half a pint or a pint of milk into the customer's jug as the milkman's dirty sleeve hovered perilously close to the milk. The baker also used a horse-drawn cart and the dustcarts and coalcarts were pulled by huge dray horses. Dustmen walked through every house to collect the dustbin from the back garden and then returned it empty the same way. Galvanised dustbins were very heavy to lift. The dustmen wore very strong sacking made into a hood and flowing right down. This provided protection for their backs while carrying the bins. The rag and bone man too had a horse and cart. He shouted for old clothes and furniture. His horse always stopped outside a certain house and mounted the pavement to peer over the front garden hedge. The horse would not move until the front door opened and a child appeared carrying two slices of bread and marmalade. The same horse would also stand outside a sweet shop until his master bought some dolly mixtures for him to eat. I guess the horse had a very sweet tooth.

Grace Smith-Grogan

Open-topped Buses

Some Sunday mornings we used to get a bus to Brixton to go to the Christian Science church. I didn't really understand the

A No. 84 tram travels past the bombed King's Arms at Peckham Rye.

An electric train waits at Peckham Rye Station in August 1955.

service but it didn't matter where you went because the service was always the same. I liked the Christian Science Monitor paper as it had a children's page with a picture article. I think it was Milly Molly Mandy. The journey to Brixton was enjoyable in the open-topped buses. If it was raining we would sit on the floor under the waterproof cover that was fitted to the seats. The bus we used was the No. 37 to Brixton. We used a No. 536 bus, which was a private bus service, to Catford where my grandmother lived. It was a brown bus.

One Christmas we were taken over to my mother's father in Finsbury Park and the snow was so thick I had to be carried over the roads.

Barbara Kennedy

Buses Dropped Hot Ash

Although I was born in Bermondsey, my earliest memory is of living at Peckham in Brayards Road. This was in about 1912, the year the *Titanic* was sunk. Peckham was an exciting place to live in. The famous Rye was close at hand, providing a superb arena for cricket, football and rounders, and also donkey rides. A little further afield was One Tree Hill with its wonderful view of London. Then there was Rye Lane which was like Aladdin's Cave. Two enormous stores, Jones & Higgins and Holdron's, dominated by amusement arcades, the Penny Bazaar, and the fantastic Tower Cinema reputed to be the largest in Europe. Along this magical thoroughfare went the last of the horse buses to be followed by the National steam bus. This friendly monster traversed Rye

Lane, depositing at intervals a generous pile of red hot ash. At night the glow of the fire from the undercarriage would be reflected on the road beneath. The steam bus survived the First World War, but not by much. Thomas Tilling followed with Frank Pickup's petrol-electric omnibus and shared passengers with the famous London General B bus. Those were the days!

Walter Veale

Changing Rails

Tram cars rocked slightly from side to side as they went along. There was great interest when the driver jumped down to change the points. He used a long lever so the tram could move over to another set of rails.

Grace Smith-Grogan

Trains were Reliable

I remember when trams rattled along Queen's Road and Peckham High Street on their way to Victoria or the Embankment, and I recall the excitement when the old open-tops were replaced by smart trams with a covered-in top deck. This also applied to the buses operated by the London General Omnibus Company, or maverick companies such as City Bus Co. These would fight to get to the bus stop first, in order to pick up the waiting passengers. This was before the days of the London Passenger Transport

An Evan Cook pantechnicon crashed into Church House, St Saviour's church hall in Copleston Road, in March 1963.

Reg Cordwell cycles along Everthorpe Road in about 1950 – without a car in sight!

Board, later to become London Transport. I sometimes travelled to work by train from Queen;s Road Station to London Bridge and my recollections are that the service given by Southern Railway was perfectly reliable, which cannot always be said for today's private railway companies – or am I allowing distance to lend enchantment to my memories?

Joan Brown

Canal Was Magical

Occasionally my Uncle Bob, who was out of work at the time (he later became a bus driver), would take me for a walk to see his family who lived in Pennack Road. At Rye Lane we turned left and walked along the canal. It had a magical feel about it with lots of barges and men in peaked caps and navy blue jerseys. To me they were sailors. The shops along the way were old and quaint. One sweet shop, where they made their own sweets, had very twisty steps down to its entrance, such as I have never seen since. It was a very close community. The pavement and houses ran closely along the canal but sadly there were accidents and drownings. At the Rye Lane entrance to the canal, coaches were parked advertising day trips to the seaside, the races and holidays. The destinations and prices were displayed on blackboards.

Kathleen Adams

Canal was an Attraction

For a pre-war child born in Peckham [in 1926], an ever-enticing lure was the Cut which ran alongside our street, Rosemary Road. Its better known appellation was the 'Surrey Canal'. The houses built this side of the tow path were addressed as Boat House Walk.

In spite of constant warnings and threats from parents, children would defy them and frequent the canal edges, complete with makeshift fishing tackle: jam jars, penny fishing nets on canes, bent pins on cotton, etc. The sought after prey was sticklebacks and red throats. Like proper anglers, our booty was not always live catches, as unsavoury objects were often hauled to the surface. These were not acceptable to the nasal and visual senses and could be classified as 'unmentionables'. Apart from the possible hazards of drowning, contamination from the turgid waters, and parental threats, it required a constant look out for patrolling 'Cut Rangers' employed by the Port of London Authority. These fearsome persons were more respected than the police. They would, if you were caught, cuff you across the neck – and worse still confiscate your valuable and hard-acquired fishing tackle. In spite of these temporary drawbacks, we would at every chance be re-enticed back to the magnet of the Cut. It is sad to say that the murky menace claimed its victims: youngsters, vagrants and suicidal persons. Although this was regrettable, they were soon forgotten, for in that age children died young with diphtheria, TB, scarlet fever and so on. However, the canal was also noted for exciting moments, such as when horse-drawn strings of barges were laboriously hauled to the bank-side timber merchants, saw mills and chemical factories which flourished all the way to Peckham's Canal Head in one direction and Wells Way in the other. Quite often the barges would halt at a quaint towpath pub called the Montpelier on Boat House Walk. This was a signal for us children to clamber on and off the barges and approach those massive power-structured creatures – the horses. As a bonus the bargees, whilst quaffing their well-earned pint, let us water and feed these treasured steeds. If we were lucky our animal friends would provide us with a bucket or two of an end product which we would trade with a back-yard tomato grower in exchange for a few coppers. Although there were quite a lot of drownings, we youngsters who survived had some narrow escapes. At the age of nine while fishing, I fell in and got out of my depth, became unconscious and luckily was saved by a Boat House Walk resident. All I can recall was being dried out and put to bed by 3.30 pm by an irate Mum, who gave me a thorough hiding, and stopped my pocket money. I couldn't understand why I was punished when nearly drowning and full of disease-ridden canal water. But many years later it dawned on me that she was as frightened as I was – because the week before my dear Dad had died and one shock was more than enough for a widow with four school age children. I now fully understand her apparent anger.

During the war in the Blitz in our Peckham area, we suffered much from bombing. In spite of the total blackout, on moonlit nights the canal glistened and we residents believed that the enemy aircraft mistook the water as a railway track and bombed accordingly. Later on Lord Haw Haw, the British traitor in Germany, broadcast that the Peckham area would get special attention from the German bombers.

Since the Surrey Canal has been absorbed or swallowed up by Burgess Park, quite often while strolling in this vicinity and appreciating the modernisation of the area, I feel nostalgic leanings. As always one yearns for the good things in the past – conveniently overlooking the unpleasant happenings. As some sage said, 'The clock cannot be put back in reality, only in the mind.'

Norman Burrows

CHAPTER 5

Shops and Other Businesses

Rye Lane took over from the High Street as Peckham's principal shopping street. It became known as the Golden Mile.

The Co-op Divi'

My mother used to get mutuality club coupons from the Co-op which meant that for every pound she asked for, she had to pay back a shilling a week. This was the only way she could afford to clothe us. When my mother bought our clothes she received metal checks to the value of the clothes we bought. We enjoyed counting up the tin coins we got when buying things. At the end of the year my mother received the divi' on the total number of checks she paid in. This was added to her share capital. One time I was allowed to choose a pair of shoes so had black patent leather ankle strap shoes. These I had to clean with milk. I was only allowed to wear them as best shoes. Apart from those, I always had lace up shoes. Another thing I remember was that my father went around all our mattresses on the beds with

Jones and Higgins, founded in 1867, was Peckham's leading store until it closed in 1980.

a Flit sprayer. This was because of all the bugs that were in the walls. They could have got into the mattresses so prevention was better than cure. I don't remember ever being bitten.

Barbara Kennedy

Peckham's Oxford Street

There was excitement on Saturday nights when shops stayed open very late. Rye Lane would be awash with people walking right across the narrow main road so that the small amount of traffic struggled to pass. Street cries intermingled with one another. The fishmonger sold off his fish because there were no fridges, just blocks of ice dripping on to the pavement. He would pile up fish on fish into newspaper shouting, 'Come on gels six pennorth the lot.'

In Woolworth's at Easter time it was fascinating to watch the shop assistants pipe icing sugar flowers and Christian names on to chocolate eggs. The two big department stores, Holdron's and Jones & Higgins, held wonderful linen sales twice a year. Jones and Higgins' employed no local girls only young lady assistants who lived outside Peckham. They were expected to 'live in' over the shop. There were also 'floor walkers' in their round tailed frock coats, with a flower in the button hole. They were called by each assistant to check customers' bills and to sign them with a flourish.

The Co-op had a shuttle which was sent around the store to the cash desk. The customer's money and bill were placed in a small container, the lid screwed on then a chain was pulled down and it went whizzing along. The cashier unscrewed it, placed the change and receipt into it and sent it back. How we children loved to witness this over and over again. I remember as a toddler

The firm of M. Manze is well known for its pies. It was started by Italian immigrants who came to England in the nineteenth century.

These two cafes were photographed in December 1976.

walking around the Penny Bazaar and being frustrated because I could not see the top of the counters. I was lifted up from time to time to view the wondrous display of goods all for one penny each.

Hutton's was a fish and chip shop situated opposite The Heaton Arms and run by an old-fashioned family. The fish was fried above an enormous coal fire constantly being stoked up like the steam engines of old. A man on the side in full view of the customers made the batter and coated beautiful pieces of fish before slipping them into the bubbling fat. Customers could eat on the premises while sitting in high-backed seats, like church pews, with tables sunk into the floor. Fish costing 2d, 3d or 4d could be bought with a pennyworth of chips. The aroma was delicious and the shop was always crowded.

Our family and friends always sat around a long table at home every Saturday evening to enjoy a lovely Hutton's fish and chip supper. I could list so many more wonderful shops which made Rye Lane the Oxford Street of Peckham. At night it was lit up by tasteful neon lights over every shop.

Grace Smith-Grogan

Rye Lane was a Fairyland

I feel the true picture of Peckham in the 1920s, 1930s and 1940s should be known. To compare the present Peckham to the old one is a travesty as the present Peckham is but a shadow of its former self. Rye Lane was a fairyland of wonderful shops with three cinemas and two excellent large stores, Jones & Higgins

and Holdrons. The shops all displayed their merchandise with taste and pride and in the evenings all were ablaze with lights. In fact, Peckham Rye was then the place to be. Besides the open-air swimming pool, it boasted a paddling pool, a dog pond near the bandstand, at which various bands played every Sunday evening. The park was a veritable Kew Gardens, beautifully laid out and attended, with nice tennis courts and one could walk the streets in safety. How do I know all this? Well, I was brought up in Melon Road. I was a member of the 48th Camberwell Scout Group and eventually became the cubmaster. I was also a member of the Bradfield Club, for whom I boxed many times. The school played cricket on the Rye once a week, swimming galas were a regular feature at Dulwich Baths and near the east side of the Rye there was a permanent fair known as Wilson's. Comparing the present day Peckham with the old one is like putting Petticoat Lane on a par with Bond Street! Pre-war Peckham was a joy to behold and an Aladdin's Cave of wonderful shops, cinemas and people – that was the real Peckham.

Bill Payne (1991)

Christmas Grotto

Rye Lane was our main shopping centre and you could shop there at almost any time of the day. In the evening the Lane would have stalls at the roadside, which were lit with oil or acetylene lamps, selling mostly foodstuffs with stallholders vying with one another in loud voices on the cheapness of their goods. The time I remember best was at Christmas when we went down the Lane with father who carried a large Gladstone bag which we filled with fruit, nuts, dates and figs to decorate the sideboard on Christmas Day. It was a great time to visit stores like Jones & Higgins and also Holdron's where they usually had a grotto set up with Father Christmas giving out presents to children. There was lots of activity in Peckham on Christmas morning, but soon after 3 p.m. all the buses and trams stopped and the Rye was deserted as everyone settled down to their Christmas festivities.

Charles J.A. Preuveneers

A Cheap Joint

On Saturday nights my mother would go to the butcher's in Choumert Road and the butcher would be shouting, 'Come buy now'. Mother would get her joint much cheaper then – at about 9 p.m. No shops are like that today.

Myrtle Newman

Work at Holdron's

When I was fourteen I left school and found a job as a cashier at Holdron's in Rye Lane. This was the big deparment store that went from Bournemouth Road and Copeland Road to the railway arch and Rye Lane. When I first worked there it was quite awe-inspiring as there were two long corridors leading to Rye Lane and there were commissionaires on the doors. The junior cashiers were in small boxes similar to a telephone box and there was one in every department. The main cash desk dealt with special sales of club vouchers, hire purchase and petty cash. Next to this was a post office counter. When Holdron's had a sale, the doors were kept locked until it was time for the rush to begin – and what a rush it was! People came from everywhere and we were quite frightened as we could have been knocked over in our cash boxes.

There was a Gown Department. This was where the more expensive dresses were sold and juniors were not allowed to go there unless they had to deliver a message. Also we were not allowed to go through the shop during the lunch hour. We had to go to the staff entrance in Bournemouth Road. There was a doorkeeper and we had to leave our shopping bags with him and go upstairs to the cloakroom and clock in. When we left we had to clock out. After a while I was promoted to a Senior Cashier. I had been working only five months when the Second World War broke out. I really wanted to go into the Forces but I couldn't, as I am blind in one eye due to an accident as a child. So I had to stay at Holdron's during all the war years. In fact I stayed until it closed down in 1949. I was married by then. My husband also worked for Holdron's but he worked outside in the Despatch Department. This was where goods were parcelled up and despatched to customers. When I first joined the firm it belonged to Selfridge's but it changed hands and became part of the John Lewis Partnership. It was sad when Holdron's closed. We could really do with another store like it now.

Doris Daniels

The Tailor's Macaw

My brother Jack used to work in a tailor's shop in Rye Lane – Sydney Fox. To attract attention and get more customers, they had a macaw in the window. It was a beautiful bird with lovely colours. After it had been in the window for three months we had it at home for another three months after which it went back to the shop. We used to laugh because it would say: 'Come on Jack – time to get up'. Mother was glad when the three months were up as it made such a mess in the parlour.

Myrtle Newman

Suit Taken to Pawnbroker's

At the Peckham Rye end of Rye Lane was a pawnbroker. My mum would take something in – usually dad's suit, for five shillings. Also in Rye Lane was Kennedy's shop which was famous for their fish and bloater paste, sausages and pies all made in their factory in Peckham. I worked in that factory for a while and I worked very hard. As compensation, a house owned by the Kennedy family, which was on the Isle of Wight at Sandown, was used as a holiday home for any family or worker who had been ill or wanted a holiday.

Marina M. Clayton (née Morris)

Nunhead Shops

There were few shops near Tresco Road where I was born. We relied on Castle's Stores in Waveney Avenue – a real 'village' store run by old Mr Castle and his assistant. There was not much pre-packaged food in those days. I remember how Mr Castle used to fold blue sheets of paper into cones and fill them with tea or sugar from large drawers at the back of the counter. On the corner of New James Street in Nunhead Lane stood Hammond's newsagent's shop where we collected our comics on Saturday morning. We used to go to the post office in Nunhead Green and buy a 1d stamp each week, and when we had collected twelve they were exchanged for a 1/- stamp. When we had collected sixteen of these we were able to buy our first National Savings Certificate. In the newsagent's I would buy grandfather's tobacco called Nosegay which then cost $7\frac{1}{2}$d an ounce.

Charles J.A. Preuveneers

Choumert Road Market

I remember the hustle and bustle of the thriving market in Choumert Road. I remember particularly the fishmonger, Lew Jacobs, calling his offer, 'Thruppence a pair of kippers,' etc. The butcher auctioned off his stock late on Saturday afternoon – a joint of beef unwrapped and then, with the same hand, a leg of lamb or hand of pork.

Dorothy Walmsley

Carter's Furniture Survives

I look back with nostalgia when the name A. Carter & Son (Home Furnishers) is mentioned – a double-fronted shop whose window display of attractive solid oak and walnut furniture invited curiosity. Mr Carter, then later his son, would stand in the entrance smiling and chatting pleasantly to passers-by. In 1940 I purchased a solid golden oak dining room suite and walnut veneered bedroom suite, among other items. A war bride in 1941, I arranged the furniture in our new home. Fifty-eight years later it is still in residence, having survived the war and stresses and strains of family life.

Grace Smith-Grogan

Jones & Higgins was for the Posh

There were popular shops in Rye Lane – Home & Colonial and Lipton's (both grocery shops), a draper's called Ghinns where I bought my first stockings (lisle at 6¾d) and Holdron's. If you were posh you went to the large Jones & Higgins' store.

Marina M.Clayton (née Morris)

Shopping Before Supermarkets

There were no supermarkets in the 1940s and 1950s in Peckham. Shopping was done in local stores and markets. The covered market, close to what is now Argos, is a pale shadow of the bustling, thriving market that I remember. Opposite was Sainsbury's; you can still see the tiled frontage and windows which now form the frontage of a shoe shop. Instead of large supermarkets and superstores, we had a number of smaller grocery stores, as

well as Sainsbury's. Maypole, International and the Co-op competed for our trade. Kennedy's is probably the only shop to have retained the old identity. Sadly, they no longer sell their own-brand fish paste.

Choumert Road was the open street market, which it still is, but Jacobs fishmongers, Parkins newspaper shop and Mackay Bros. bacon shop have all gone. There was another covered market where Netto's now stands. From Jones & Higgins in the north to the Co-op department store in the south, Rye Lane was renowned for its shopping. What are my memories of shopping in Rye Lane? The grand staircase of Jones & Higgins where I imagined myself in The Ziegfeld Follies; descending the stairs so elegantly and then tripping down the last few steps in my first pair of high-heeled shoes! The silver service elegance of the restaurant, and the superior service that we associate only with Knightsbridge today. Jones & Higgins was in the Victorian tradition of family-run department stores such as Swan & Edgar, Bourne & Hollingsworth and Chiesman's of Lewisham. Although Jones & Higgins tried to become up-to-date, it lost its identity when it became the Houndsditch of Peckham and never recovered.

The J. Lyons teashops were where ordinary people had tea or lunch while they shopped; there were two in Rye Lane. There was also a Black & White milk bar and later a Wimpy bar. The Co-op also had a restaurant where my mother and grandmother took me to lunch when I was only four or five years old. They ordered toad-in-the-hole and I screamed the place down, refusing to eat toads. My family never let me live it down. I think the restaurant closed down soon afterwards. Also at the south end of Rye Lane I can remember Cullens who sold fresh ground coffee (an unusual taste in those days) and spices from open racks. They also sold raisins and sultanas that had to be washed and de-stalked. The smell of that shop was unbelievable – the mingled smells of coffee and spices.

My mother worked at a large draper's called Davey Bros. which was in Rye Lane between Sternhall Lane and Nigel Road. Customers would hand their money to the assistants and it would be sealed, with the sale slip which had been written out specifying the items purchased, and placed in a tube which was then whizzed along on an overhead wire to the cashier. How did it know which wire would return it to the right assistant? The ceiling was criss-crossed with these tubes whooshing back and forth. The Co-op had a similar but more sophisticated system. The money and sales slip would be sealed in the tube but sent through tubes by vacuum suction. We did our daily shopping in Choumert Market or Bellenden Road, where there was a Co-op grocer, baker and butcher. Tea was bought in $\frac{1}{4}$lb packets of thick sugar paper. Every last tea leaf was shaken out and the packet opened to ensure that nothing remained. We were not well off and the war had made people careful to use all they had without waste.

Only as a last resort would we buy firewood, from the shop in Choumert Road nicknamed the oil shop. It smelt of creosote and paraffin but also sold hardware, brooms, tools etc. I can remember my first banana, unobtainable during the war, and many other items were hard to get. Luxuries like oranges and bananas were kept under the counter for favoured customers.

Norma Francis

Chopped up Live Eels

We did a lot of walking around the streets with friends. We went past Kennedy's large shop, which sold sausages, pies, fish paste and many other things. Some of the nicest sausages were the Cambridge ones which were a mixture of pork and beef. We also bought salmon and shrimp paste in small or large cartons with no lids on them. Sometimes we bought bloater paste but I didn't like this very much because it was too salty. The shop was near the workshops for blind people in Peckham Road. This was a large building where blind people made cane baskets and other things. Another shop that we used to go to was the Maypole Dairy which was in Rye Lane past Jones & Higgins. It was great to see the assistants pat up the butter, either in rolls or flat packs. I always had to get margarine and a little butter, which was put on to our bread – just a scraping of butter on top of the margarine. My brother did not like this so we always had to get Mayqueen for him. I don't know why he had to be different. I think the Mayqueen was margarine and a percentage of butter mixed together.

Another shop that was fascinating was a corn chandler's. They sold a lot of dried goods like peas and butter beans. These were in sacks on the floor. Whatever you wanted, an assistant weighed it and put it into a cone-shaped piece of paper which the staff made up themselves after weighing the goods. Another interesting

Lilian Burden was brought up by her aunty and uncle. Uncle Charles Smith was an undertaker with premises at 15 Queen's Road. Lilian was about six when this photograph was taken.

shop was the double-fronted fish shop on the corner of Hill Street. It had all sorts of fish on one side of the shop window. The other side had a tray of eels crawling over each other. I didn't like the way they chopped them up when someone wanted some, still alive.

Barbara Kennedy

Raced through Austin's

There was a furniture store and warehouse with a lot of chairs and couches outside. That was Austin's where we could race through and sit on everything before being chased off.

Marina M. Clayton (née Morris)

Black Market Nylons

Rye Lane is always remembered with great affection – Jones & Higgins, Holdron's, Wharlton's (high class fruiterers), Ghinns 2 $\frac{3}{4}$ d Lisle stockings and the Arcade where we bought black market nylons during the last war. I didn't know they were black market at the time. We were so innocent. We even waited for a receipt and couldn't understand why the stallholder fell about laughing. Also in Rye Lane I remember Lucille Gay where, for many years I had my hair done. Christmas was a wonderful time – the shops looked wonderful.

Peggy Lovett

Newman's Christmas Cake

Near the southern end of Rye Lane there was a butcher's where there were live animals at Christmas. Cows, and possibly sheep, were kept in a yard at the side of the shop. Further down, near the Peckham Rye Tabernacle, was Newman's baker's shop where at Christmas they had a Christmas cake with so many tiers that it reached the ceiling in the shop.

Lilian Burden (born 1901)

Rye Lane Sold Everything

Rye Lane bustled with people and traffic. Every side road and odd space had a stall selling something. The stall at the exit to the coal yard had to be moved out of the way when a horse-drawn coal cart came out of the yard, which was opposite the station. The customers patiently waited to be served. Flares lit the stalls on the dark days. They gave a very bright light that hissed a bit but generally brightened up our world. I think it was in Elm Grove that an elderly Italian gentleman sold ice cream; one ha'penny bought you a cornet of lemon ice. It was lovely and never to be forgotten. Jones & Higgins and Holdron's were top-class departmental stores with liveried commissionaires. During the year they would have various exhibitions. The building of the Sydney Harbour was one I remember. Personalities of the day would visit and I saw Jean Batten the aviator. They even had a flea circus which was quite popular, poor little fleas. Christmas displays were wonderful for children. A ride to visit Father Christmas could be by a sleigh through fairyland or in a submarine with the fishes swimming around. Choumert Road was where all the mums went looking for a cheap nourishing meal for their families. It had lots of stalls including butchers, greengrocers and a bustling fish shop. On Christmas Eve it was packed with people as the butchers sold the poultry cheaper – very few freezers then. On the corner a little old lady sold second-hand books; she was a permanent feature.

We loved the music of the barrel organs. It cheered everyone up and brought a smile to all the faces. I did not like the troupe of dancing men dressed and made up like women. They were weird and grubby. I went the long way round to avoid them. They scared me. Everybody shopped in Woolworth's, the 'nothing over sixpence' shop. Most of our homes came from there – saucepans, kettles, sheet music, tools, screws and nails, sweets, cooking pans, biscuits, cups and saucers, plates of all sizes, pens, pencils, notepaper, and such a variety of choice. All their stores had the same atmosphere with their wooden floors and island counters displaying their wares. You never waited very long to be served as the shop assistant was behind the counter to take your money. I did all my present shopping there. Marks & Spencer was more upmarket, nothing over five shillings. I don't remember buying anything in there as a child. The covered market was always worth a visit for a bargain. We looked forward to the British Home Stores being built next to the Scotch Wool Shop. Further along was Morgan and Collins, a large haberdashers. Ghinns was the wool shop where we bought knitting wool for our gloves and jumpers at two pence an ounce. Rye Lane

George Austin, founder of G. Austin & Sons, stands in front of his premises in Brayards Road. Three perambulator-type milk floats and two horse-drawn milk carts are lined up in the road outside Oxford Farm Dairy.

had a wonderful selection of shops selling dresses, shoes, radios – anything and everything, if you had the money. Our shopping done and money gone we would go home. The shopping bags were heavy – no baskets on wheels in those days. Home to the special treat, which we had bought for our tea.

Kathleen Adams

Jones & Higgins had Shop Walkers

On the right-hand side of Queen's Road, under the railway bridge at Queen's Road Peckham station was a fairly large Royal Arsenal Co-operative Society store where I used to do my mother's shopping on a Saturday morning. I seem to remember there was sawdust on the floor and that I was given tin 'coins' as a dividend on what I spent.

In the row of shops on the other side of the road to the RACS store there was one called Whomes. I think their main business was selling pianos but they also sold 78 speed vinyl records. Inside the shop were cardboard boxes of second-hand records and among them I remember finding the first jazz record I ever bought. It cost me sixpence and was a recording of the Benny Goodman Trio. I was about fourteen at the time and now, over sixty years later, I still play and enjoy recordings by that Trio. In fact, on a compact disc I have two tracks that were on my ten-inch sixpenny vinyl recording.

At the end of Queen's Road on the

right, opposite Queen's Road Methodist church, was a large men's and boys' outfitters. I can't remember the name of the shop but it sold the blazers, caps etc. worn by boys at Wilson's Grammar School in Camberwell.

When my mother wanted to shop in a department store we occasionally went to Chiesman's in Lewisham, but much more often we went to Jones & Higgins in Rye Lane. I recall it from a very early age impressing me as a wonderfully ordered store. In each department you were usually greeted by a supervisor – known as a Shop-Walker – who introduced you to an assistant. The assistants always seemed eager to serve customers and seemed well-versed in what they were selling. If a purchase could not be arranged quickly you were invited to sit by the glass-topped counters on bentwood chairs with cane seats. My mother always claimed that Jones & Higgins was the best shop for blue serge – a material out of which most of the suits I wore as a boy were made. I accompanied my mother to a number of other shops in Rye Lane including Holdron's, another department store. We also went to Sainsbury's which by comparison with today's superstores was a very small shop. It was a change to go to Sainsbury's because in New Cross we had a David Greig's shop. It was said that David Greig and John Sainsbury were friends and that since they sold similar products they agreed never to compete with each other in the same area. Other shops used by my mother were Timpson's, where my first pair of football boots were purchased and the RACS clothing shop. From the latter came the suit I wore when, at the age of sixteen, I started work at a London Clearing Bank. It was a black coat and vest with striped trousers but I didn't think I looked anything like so distinguished as our family doctor. Perhaps it was because he wore spats.

My parents always bought second-hand rather than new furniture. They maintained it was better quality. As a result we went to the store of G. Austin at Peckham Rye and to their warehouse in Brayards Road from time to time. I can remember gazing with something approaching awe at the beautifully made and handsome pieces of Victorian and Edwardian furniture. It filled me with a determination that one day I would be able to buy such things.

Norman Lenton

Naphtha Flares

Choumert Road, famous for its market stalls, was lit up by naphtha flares, glowing through the murky, foggy mists of winter. I hear their hissing sound now. Braziers of orange-red coke invited all to stop by and warm frozen fingers. Traders used Cockney rhyming slang to sell their wares with a saucy, 'Come on gels, winter draws on'. The salad stall had small round lettuces costing two for 1d and punnets of mustard and cress for 4d. The sweet stall sold delicious pink and white coconut ice and fudge sliced up in dainty pieces. Rock hard cough candy, so very warming on a cold day, was broken into small pieces with a little hammer. The cat meat stall had great chunks of sliced horse flesh, which had a sweet sickly smell, savoured by a few stray cats, miaowing below and hoping for a piece to drop. The haberdashery stall sold cottons, ribbons

Men chat outside Ascott's photographic shop in Rye Lane in October 1961.

and lace which were measured by the yard – the tip of a nose to the end of an outstretched arm. A short arm was not popular with customers. A small open barrow was presided over by a frail little lady in an old-fashioned dress. Dog-eared paperback books were exchanged for a penny or two. There was a flower stall where, when I was fourteen, I could buy three daffodils for 2d out of my week's wages to take home for my mother. I remember her delight as she placed them in a slim vase in the centre of the table.

There was an eel and pie shop where a crowd would gather to watch the macabre spectacle of eels being chopped up live – the only way they were allowed to be sold.

Sometimes a hand would be bitten and blood would stream down. It was a ghastly sight. People would, without any concern while sitting on high-backed benches with small tables, enjoy jellied eels or a pie and mash with generous spoonfuls of eels liquor made into a parsley gravy.

Grace Smith-Grogan

I Hated Shopping

Saturday afternoon for my parents was for shopping and we would cut through 'the back doubles' to Rye Lane. There was a proliferation of stalls selling all manner of goods. My father had a particular stall where he would stock up with fruit, which was cheap and 'good for us'. I can see him now with a carrier bag at his feet, which he would fill for a few pence.

Choumert Road was my preference as on one stall there were toffee apples for sale, all freshly made with plenty of toffee. I did not always get one bought for me but I always lived in hope. Another stall sold rabbit joints and my mother, who was an excellent cook, could produce a delicious rabbit stew for just a few pence. My mother was also a first-class seamstress and knitter and more often than not a visit to Ghinns down Rye Lane was a must to stock up on wool. We went to Holdron's store for cheap materials. Another shop which was nearly always visited was Kennedy's. This shop was famous for its fish and meat paste; for a rare treat we would get some of its sausages. I disliked shopping day but, much as I pleaded to be let off, I had to go with them. Once they did relent and left me behind after being told to behave

A totter kept his horse and cart in a yard off Carlton Grove in October 1971.

myself or 'never again'. During the afternoon I climbed a tree and fell out, fracturing and dislocating my right elbow which meant a trip to King's College Hospital. This put me out of action for several weeks. I was never allowed to stay behind again. I was six at the time.

Generally speaking, my mother let me go out on my own with friends and apart from this one time I came to no harm, although I had a narrow squeak while investigating what we all called the haunted empty house, which was on the site where later the Pioneer Health Centre was built. We had ranged from room to room until on the upper floor we came upon a food service lift or dumb waiter. Being adventurous, I climbed in and asked my friends to lower me down by the rope, the device for lowering and raising the lift with food. Unfortunately I was too heavy and they could not hold me and I plummeted down to the bottom with a thump which knocked my breath out. But that was all – another lesson learned.

Harold Elven

Worked at Samuel Jones

Before my marriage I worked for Samuel Jones Engineering Co. I well remember the lovely Camberwell Beauty on the main building and the little shops in Southampton Way. My mind also goes back to the corn chandler's on the corner of Havil Street where we used to buy white china eggs to put under our hens to encourage them to lay. The Chocolate Box sold a mouth-watering selection of high class chocolates. There was a little greengrocer's and florist's shop where my wedding bouquet

and floral headdress were made. Unfortunately they forgot to take my address with the order so there was pandemonium in Peckham on my wedding day! Eventually I got to the church on time complete with bouquet and a rather battered headdress. I married in Rye Lane Chapel in 1952 and we lived in Crofton Road. Our daughter was born in 1955 in St Giles' Hospital. The treatment there was horrendous and would not be tolerated today. My daughter went to Oliver Goldsmith School where I had been a pupil.

I would like to mention 'Mary' who had a salad stall to the left of Jones & Higgins. I will never forget her kindness and generosity to me when I was a one parent family. Her kindness has been passed on many times. I left Peckham in 1964 and although I have lived in Hampshire for thirty-five years, my roots are still in Peckham even though it has changed so dramatically during that time. I still wallow in nostalgia every time I receive *Peckham Society News* for which I thank the hard working committee of The Peckham Society.

Peggy Lovett

Cows in Lugard Road

On returning from evacuation to Henley-on-Thames during the last war, my family lived at 32 Lugard Road and we bought our milk from the dairy in our road. It was a bustling little road. As well as the cows and prefabs, three shops and a kiosk have also gone. There was an off-licence opposite a grocer's on the corner of Kirkwood Road. On the corner of Caulfield Road Mr Nimmo had a dear little newsagent's where, from the age of eleven to sixteen, I did a seven-day a week paper round. (I went to work when I was fifteen.) Just before the bustling Evan Cook's was a kiosk in which served a most dignified lady. The derelict wooden shutters of the kiosk are still there; the shops are now houses. There was always activity around the prefabs which were inhabited by families with children playing outside, in the pre-television age, and in the front gardens of the prefabs with their two attractive lime trees either side of the wooden gates. The demise of the street life along with the loss of the shops is regrettable.

Valerie Newman

A Dreaded Shed

A dairy which had its own herd of cattle was situated via a short alley at 51a Lugard Road. This was Jorden's. If you were unlucky, you could be sent up to ask for a bucket of manure at very little or no cost but it had to be retrieved yourself from a large smelly shed!

Ray Byfield

Peckham Cows

There was a dairy in Lugard Road and we used to get our milk there. We enjoyed seeing the cows being milked. We knew their names – Daisy, Marigold and other names I have forgotten. The cows were there for a week and then taken to the country when a fresh lot would replace them. The milk was delicious.

Myrtle Newman

Mrs Alice Anson, Vera Conway's grandmother, is seen here with Toby the cat in the back garden at 9 Haslam Place.

Bird Cages Factory

There was a little factory in Middle Street which made bird cages where many boys worked after they left school at fourteen. My two brothers worked there.

Nellie Thornton

Great Grandfather Ropemaker

The address that was special to our family was 9 Haslam Place. My grandmother lived there with her mother and father. She was the youngest of ten and always said that she was an 'afterthought'. Gran's father was a ropemaker and carried on his business in a shed in the garden. He had a horse which was stabled out there too and so it was led through the house at the end of the day. The ropes were made from hemp. Local children were never short of ropes for skipping in the street, nor were they short of pipes for blowing bubbles as another neighbour's business was to make pipes. Great grandfather was illiterate so if he ever needed to sign his name – as he did when pensions were introduced – he just put a cross for his mark. Towards the end of his life, he suffered from dementia and would still leave the house in the morning with the intention of selling his ropes but would get lost, forget where he lived and was often brought home by people who knew him well as a trader.

Vera Conway

Street Bargains

Between the wars there were real 'Derek Trotters' who appeared as if by magic to open their suitcases of never-to-be-repeated bargains and who disappeared just as quickly when the ever vigilant bobby came on the scene.

Dorothy Walmsley

Sunday Trade

Every Sunday morning a man with a cart used to come around Peckham with salt and vinegar for sale. It was 1½d for a three-cornered block of salt and 2d for a pint of vinegar. He also sold grey and white hearthstone as well as bundles of firewood

Price & Co. (Bakers) Ltd used a horse and cart for deliveries in Copleston Road in May 1955.

A tram and a bus proceed east along Peckham High Street with two cyclists heading west in the early 1950s.

for ld each. He did a good trade.

Nellie Thornton

Grandfather was a Builder

My maternal grandfather was a builder and builders' merchant, opposite Peckham Rye common, around 1870-1900, on the corner of Nunhead Lane and subsequently in the Old Kent Road until about 1904 when he took a lease on a house and industrial premises in Commercial Road (now Way).
I moved away from Peckham when I was a child but I visited Nunhead Cemetery in the 1960s while it was still privately owned though mainly closed to new burials.

Leonard Phillips

Cattle on the Streets

Cattle were herded on to the corner of Choumert Road and Victoria (now Bellenden) Road and then taken to a slaughterhouse in Reedham Street.

Vera Constable

CHAPTER 6

Street Life

A street party was held in Manaton Road in June 1953 to celebrate the coronation.

Street Life

On New Year's Eve everyone stood at their front doors at midnight and welcomed neighbours over the threshold with pieces of coal and bread. Old feuds were forgotten. Another occasion when folk stood at their front doors was on Sunday mornings. The familiar sounds of the Boys' Brigade band brought everyone out on the street. There was a great air of expectation and pride as

they marched past playing rousing music. On Sundays the muffin man came around the streets. We all wanted to ring his loud handbell and marvelled at the way he balanced the large tray of muffins on his head. The shellfish man sold us winkles and shrimps which were a regular Sunday teatime treat which we enjoyed with celery and beetroot – and we always had home-made rock cakes or bread pudding as well. Throughout the year tramps and gypsies

Rye Lane full of shoppers in October 1961.

knocked on our door. We didn't have a lot but no one was turned away without a cup of tea and a slice of bread and dripping. Mother would also try to get an old pram and fill it with warm clothes and shoes for a gypsy lady called Mrs Lee who called every year in the autumn for it when the Romanies were wintering near the Rye. Among other folk I remember knocking at the door was the cats' meat man, who sold horse meat. We were regular customers. Our cats loved it but I think the man ate more than he sold!

Other people who knocked at the door were the tally man, the rag and bone man, the Italian ice cream man, the rent man, the insurance man and the milkman. Mum would never have anything on tick. If she couldn't pay for it, she went without. If a death occurred in the street, one neighbour would do a collection from every house for a wreath. On the day of the funeral all curtains would be drawn and not opened until the coffin had left the street. The coffin was usually carried in a carriage drawn by black horses which the Co-op would have arranged.

Steamrollers in the streets caused excitement. They covered the roads in smelly, sticky black tar and stones. We used to get covered in the stuff.

Peggy Lovett

Men Dressed up as Women

Men, dressed up as women, used to trudge around the streets with barrel organs. They wore the most dirty, tatty dresses, battered high heel shoes and wigs. Were they the original drag artists? They certainly entertained me and other children. The hokey-pokey man sold lumps of frozen ice with a bit of lemon for $\frac{1}{2}$d.

Margaret Chandler

Barrel Organs

What a joy was the barrel organ! Ex-servicemen did a cancan, all dressed up and with a lot of make-up. We accepted them as ex-servicemen who were all out of work. (My own dad was out of work for eight years.) We were only children but understood why men danced and dressed in frills and fancies. They needed to feed their families.

Everyone came round Copeland Avenue to enjoy the barrel organ. We lived at 6 Copeland Avenue, off Copeland Road, where there's a car park today.

Marina M. Clayton (née Morris)

Oswald Mosley in Rye Lane

I lived in Peckham from 1917 until 1942. In Rye Lane, at the Rye end, there was the triangle where there were several stalls and it was also a miniature speakers' corner; the most infamous man who came was Mosley. My mother forbade me to go there because of the Blackshirts, but I was about 12 or 13 so pushed through right up to the rostrum – just to look at this man. Mosley looked down and said, 'Go home little girl'. I went and then boasted about what I had done and got a good hiding. (It was well deserved!)

Marina M. Clayton (née Morris)

Bands Played

All litter was disposed of quickly and the pavements and roads were immaculate. Boy Scouts, Girl Guides as well as Girls' Life Brigade and Boys' Brigade members paraded through the streets behind their bands. Down the side streets people rushed to their front doors or peeped through their curtains to see the smart uniforms and fresh faces of the youngsters marching past.

There were very few street lamps but the

New electricity cables were laid in Copleston Road in May 1963.

74

A victory party was held in Chadwick Road in 1946.

lamplighter caused excitement when he pulled a lever and up popped the lighted gas lamp. Children followed him on his rounds. Muffin men, with a tray on their heads and ringing a bell, shouted: 'Muffins for sale, all fresh'. The Wall's ice cream man and his rival from Eldorado rode on their tricycles with a large blue and white box attachment full of mouth-watering ice cream. The famous Wall's slogan was, 'Stop me and buy one'. Dogs roamed freely through the streets taking themselves for a walk.

Grace Smith-Grogan

Ladies Wore Hats

Like a colourful pageant, a kaleidoscope of pictures and events crowd my mind as I look back over eighty years of life in Peckham. Masses of people walking everywhere, hardly a motor car in sight. Happy people laughing and chatting on street corners. Pretty summer dresses with a sunshade or two instead of the dark sombre trouser suits of today. Women were so feminine then. Ladies always wore hats in winter and summer. Bare heads were unknown.

Grace Smith-Grogan

Pavement Games

In the streets children played hopscotch and with hoops on the lovely York paving stones. Little girls pushed dolls prams and boys raced along on go-karts made with a plank and pram wheels.

Grace Smith-Grogan

Where's Willie Tapper?

When I was a pupil in Adys Road Infants School, my name was written on a hoarding

People board a bus in Rye Lane, opposite Jones & Higgins' store, in May 1961.

in Fenwick Road. Someone had written: 'Take notice – Willie Tapper loves Grace Yates'. I was not thrilled. Willie Tapper indeed! I wonder where he is today.

Grace Smith-Grogan (née Yates)

Counting the Coal Sacks

Half a century ago street life was not so different in many ways from today. People went to work by train or bus, shopped in Rye Lane and looked after their houses. In other ways it was a different world. Children played in the street and there were few cars before the 1960s. Front doors were left open because there were always people around, keeping an eye on the children, cleaning windows or front steps. I loved the horses that came pulling the milk wagon, coal cart or the rag and bone man. I would run indoors to beg an apple or sugar lump to give the horse, while keen gardeners would run for a bucket to retrieve the droppings for their compost heap.

Coal sacks were carried through to our coal bunker in the back garden. Some houses had coal cellars with an access hole in the front of the houses. In both cases someone had to count the sacks as they were delivered to make sure there were no mistakes. I can remember feeling very important when I was first given that responsibility.

Norma Francis

The Whistling Man

My school friend Vera and I sometimes took a stroll holding hands with Ronald Gourley, a well-known broadcaster on the radio. He was known as the 'Whistling Man' as he would whistle to music. He was blind so children would lead him. He would stop at a sweet shop known as Addison's corner opposite the King's Arms. He would buy us sugared almonds in a pretty floral paper bag. They were a great treat.

Grace Smith-Grogan

Waved a Black Handkerchief

Queen Mary was visiting Peckham in 1931 to open the Union of Girls' Schools Settlement (now The Peckham Settlement) in Stafford Street. As she was driven in her car down Peckham High Street, Queen Mary bowed regally and waved her hand to the people lining the street. My mother was standing in the front row and waved her handkerchief to the Queen as everyone else was doing. The Queen looked straight at my mother and inclined her head graciously. My mother was in the seventh heaven of delight. It was only on returning home that she realised to her horror that her handkerchief had a deep border of black. It was designed for people in mourning! Black edged notepaper and envelopes were also used in respect for the dear departed.

Grace Smith-Grogan

A piano was wheeled out into a street in June 1953 when residents of Manaton Road and Claude Road held a street party to celebrate the coronation.

CHAPTER 7

Pastimes

The swings outside Austin's were popular.

Projectionist at Tower Cinema

I was born in 1923 and attended Lyndhurst Grove School before transferring to Adys Road School. My dear Dad used to meet me every Friday on the corner of Ondine Road. It was a lovely treat to see him waiting to take me to the pictures.

He always asked me, 'Where shall we go – the Tower or the Annexe?' I preferred the Tower Cinema as we used to see actors on the stage as well as a band or organist. It was cheaper too: 6d for Dad and 4d for me. The Annexe was a miserable place and it was 10d and 6d. It was very smoky – just like a fog. I do believe that place ruined my eyes. I would love to sit and read a book for hours and hours but I have never been able to since going to the Tower Cinema Annexe.

In 1935, when I was twelve, the Tower Cinema had its twenty-first birthday and there was a lovely cake. It was so big it nearly reached the ceiling. Later I worked as a projectionist at the Tower Cinema. As I was doing a man's job, I was exempt from being called up for the forces.

Agnes Boyle

As the popularity of pubs declined, some closed including the Golddiggers Arms in Consort Road. It was converted into offices.

The Windsor Castle in Garnies Street, off Sumner Road, was demolished.

Bath Tavern is another Peckham pub which no longer exists. It was situated at 195 Asylum Road.

Part of the former entrance to the Tower Cinema in Rye Lane which was renovated by Free Form Arts Trust in 1999. Above the arched window is a verse written by Caswallon Evans:

The Pilgrims of Peckham surging forth in their might.
To Camberwell's Mecca on Saturday night,
Eager-eyed buyers keenly gauging the worth.
Of wares richly piled from the ends of the Earth;
Flaming youth gaily seeking the Temple of Fame,
And dreamy-eyed Age tramping Memory's Lane,
But lovers ecstatic will ever drift by.
In the Lane of Romance that leads to the Rye.

Wilson's Fairground

I was born in the depths of winter 1932 at 47 Melbourne Grove but when I was six weeks old we moved to Claude Road where I lived until I married in 1953. Many changes have happened since my childhood. Rye Lane is no longer the wonderful shopping centre where you could get everything you needed. I can remember my dad, Charlie Side, taking my brother Fred and myself shopping late on Saturday afternoons and in the early evening to Rye Lane and especially to Jones & Higgins and Holdron's. Wilson's fair ground was our treat on a Saturday evening. During holidays we all used to get together and go up to

Peckham Rye Park and play games, have picnics and be out nearly all day. We enjoyed sandwiches made from Kennedy's meat or fish paste.

Doreen Spence

Saw Cinema Built

While I was a pupil at Wood's Road School, I watched the Tower Cinema being built. It opened in 1914.

Lilian Burden (aged 98)

Tea and Biscuits Provided

The main cinemas in Rye Lane were the Tower and Tower Annexe. In the High Street was the Queen's Hall. We were not allowed to go in a cinema unless accompanied by an adult so we often stood outside the Annexe asking people if they would take us in. The seats were usually 3d or 6d. In the afternoon some cinemas would provide tea and biscuits for the dearer seats.

Charles J.A. Preuveneers

Tower Cinema Was Grand

There were three cinemas in Rye Lane – the Tower Annexe, the Tower and the Imperial. The Imperial held the afternoon children's matinee – 2d to go in and we had a penny for sweets. The Tower Cinema was grand. The entrance had a large staircase. Before you went to the pay box, the usherettes would take you to your seat. They would put on the news, a small film, which was followed by the main film. I saw the talkie *King of Jazz*. Instead of

people reading out loud (though some people did) we sat back to listen. Lon Chaney in the *Phantom of the Opera* frightened me; I spent most of the film hiding in my mother's lap.

Marina M. Clayton (née Morris)

Born Above Cinema

I was born at 24 High Street, above Queen's Picture Theatre, in 1922. I remember climbing out of the kitchen window, on to a flat roof of the cinema, looking over into the backyard of the doss-house next door, and seeing sheets and mattresses hanging out of the windows airing. I also remember being allowed into the projection room, and looking at the films from that vantage point. I remember too a van driving up and down the High Street advertising *All Quiet on the Western Front* in 1930. Next to the doss-house was Brown's the bakers, with a road crossing by it, which we used when going to Sumner Road School, then my sister went to Peckham Central School. I also remember the Tower Cinema and the Tower Annexe in Rye Lane. I sometimes went to the Saturday morning cinema at the Central Hall Picture Palace, which was part of the Central Hall and the Crown Working Men's Institution. We kids were given an orange, a paper comic, and sometimes sweets as well.

Barbara C. Kennedy

The Grandest Place

I have always lived in Chadwick Road, and can remember as a small child being woken on Saturday evenings particularly by the back doors of the Tower Cinema banging as the moviegoers came down the back stairs from the circle. There must have been eight doors or so across the width of Chadwick Road, which would bang one after the other as people streamed out. Then of course I would listen to their footsteps, chatter and laughter as they passed the houses. Sometimes, when we shopped in Rye Lane, we would take the short cut up the back slope lined with crush barriers for the enormous queues which formed for popular films. This led into the side entrance of the foyer, and you could then go out of the main Rye Lane entrance, saving having to push through Choumert Road market which was very busy in those days. This, however, did not prepare me for my first visit to the cinema itself. The foyer was the grandest place I had ever seen at that time. In the early evening, after school, it was ablaze with lights, there were open fires in the huge fireplaces, and pink brocade settees in the alcoves along the fifty-yard long foyer. You could have held the Vienna State Ball there. I was entranced, and can still remember that first visit as a small child. Whether or not it was quite that grand I cannot judge, but its memory has stayed with me. My parents remembered nights during the war when they sheltered in the cellars of the cinema, during air raids, as it was friendlier that way. (We had an Anderson shelter in our garden.) After the closure of the cinema, as a teenager, my friends and I would explore these same cellars which backed onto the grounds of the All Saints' church hall, and so we could gain access without being seen. We did get caught on one occasion by the local police who used to patrol on foot, and were probably after a crafty cigarette.

While recalling the Tower Cinema, I have remembered another introduction to 'gracious living' that happened in Peckham. I remember being taken to Jones & Higgins' restaurant for afternoon tea – silver service waitresses in black dresses with white-frilled aprons and caps. The tables were set with snowy white damask cloths, and flowers – even Fortnums and Harrods today could barely compete.

Norma Francis

Road Was Playground

I lived at 3 Lugard Road, the house next to Evan Cook's gates. Hollydale Primary School was my first school and Mr Draper was the headmaster. The location of all the local bomb sites became known to me and were regarded as wonderful playgrounds. The largest was the one on the corner of Lugard Road and Stanbury Road. It incorporated the ruins of many houses and also the Lugard Tavern. The site, which also had a water tank, was generally known to us as 'The Hills' because of the grassed-over mounds from the excavations of the water tank.

Lugard Road, in spite of the busy weekday Evan Cook end, was a peaceful turning in the late 1940s and 50s, and often saw a middle of the road game of cricket which would take place at the section where there was a row of prefabs. Parents often watched from their gates. The wicket was usually a metal milk crate which only on rare occasions would have to be moved because of a motorist passing through.

Ray Byfield

Big Wheel Got Stuck

At Easter time there was a fair held near the open-air swimming pool on the Rye. It had all the usual 'fun of the fair' including a Big

The corner of Lugard Road and Stanbury Road was known as 'The Hills'.

Wheel. I kept asking my mother if we could go on it but she did not want to do so. Eventually she gave way to me and we went higher and higher. When we reached the top the wheel stopped because something had gone wrong with the works. We were stuck up there for about fifteen minutes. My mother kept saying, 'Don't look down' but I did and it was frightening to see how far we were from the ground. Of course there were crowds watching us. At long last we came to earth and my dear mother said, 'No more going on that awful machine.'

Myrtle Newman

Little Gardens Created

The Courtway, or Rye Passage as it is now called, often had little squares of wild flowers, leaves and grasses laid out along one wall. These tiny gardens were made by children who said, 'Please missus remember the grotto.' A halfpenny given in gratitude was hailed with delight.

Grace Smith-Grogan

Father Was Handy

My father was very good at making things. He made a wooden stool as well as our soap and toothbrush holder. He always mended our shoes using pieces of leather he chose from a stall in East Street market. He cycled every day to work in Fulham where he worked for ShellMex.

Winifred MacKenzie (née Steel)

Standing Only

Local cinemas were always filled to capacity, with queues being the norm for a long-awaited big feature film. The last film I remember queuing for in those times was *Moby Dick* at the Regal in the Old Kent Road in 1956. I only just managed to get in for 'standing only'. The Regal was a lovely building and was my favourite cinema, the Odeon in Peckham High Street being a close second. I never went to the Tower Cinema in Rye Lane very often but I found out that Michael Caine, who attended Wilson's Grammar School, used to bunk off and go to the Tower Cinema quite frequently.

Ray Byfield

Won a Prize

I always liked to look at Austin's furniture and bric-a-brac laid out on tables. It was also fun when Wilson's fair came. Though we didn't have any money to spend, it was interesting. Wednesday was always children's day and everything was 1d so sometimes I was lucky and had a ride on the horses. Every Christmas Jones & Higgins had something special to draw the crowds. One year it was pigmies, small people from another country. Another time they had 'Uncle Bubbles'. He had a round table which was hollow in the middle and had ping pong balls in it. If you had enough money to have a go, you were given a long-handled basket and when there were enough people he started the machine which blew the ping pong balls in the air. The first person to get three balls won a prize. I was lucky to have a go once and caught three balls. I chose a box of orange crackers. We had never had anything like that before.

Barbara Kennedy

Projector Broke Down

Tower Cinema Annexe was the smallest cinema in Rye Lane. Often the projector would break down and the picture would vanish. In later years the sound would fade out. Everyone would stamp their feet, whistle and shout loudly. When the picture or sound resumed, there would be a great surge of clapping and much laughter. I believe that for the audience this was all part of the enjoyment. They would have been so disappointed if there were no breakdowns during the performance.

Grace Smith-Grogan

Fell in Pool

We loved Thursday evenings when we lived in the upstairs flat in Rye Hill Park as we could watch the Crystal Palace firework display. We could only see the rockets but it was a good show for us. One summer was hot so I went down to the boating and paddling pool next to the open-air swimming pool on Peckham Rye. It was crowded. I went paddling but fell in. I was very upset and wondered what my mother would say so I sat on the grass and took some of my clothes off and dried them on the grass. I was late home for my dinner and got told off anyway. I can never understand how we usually managed to get home in time for meals as we never had a watch. I hated meat pie. I used to go round my plate having a bit of this and a bit of that to get rid of it. Meat pie on a Sunday was all my mother could afford and if we didn't eat it we just went hungry.

Barbara Kennedy

Home Entertainment

People were often invited out to tea at weekends. They would take it in turns to entertain family and friends. If there was a pianist he or she would be expected to take music. Other people were expected to sing or recite if they had those talents. Every guest would contribute during the evening if only to tell a humorous story or relate a happening. Such happy days! My sister and I would play the piano and piano accordion. My mother would sing and in the early days play her mandolin. We were invited everywhere.

Grace Smith-Grogan

Out With Big Brother

The seven year difference between my brother Jack and me meant that we did not do a great deal together. I did look up to him and it was a treat therefore when occasionally he would take me to the open-air lido opposite the King's Arms public house. He helped me in the water because I could barely swim but as I had no fear of heights I would dive off the boards, even the highest one and brother Jack would tow me to the side of the pool.

Opposite the bus garage in Nunhead Lane, there was an area of waste ground and from time to time Wilson's fair would be set up and

I longed to go there. I was not allowed in on my own but I recall one time when Jack took me and we had a really wonderful time as he was working and had money. We did not go very often but I recall the time we both managed to have success on the Hoopla stall and won a pair of glass vases for Mum.

During weekends, particularly on Sunday afternoons, my parents would decide to go for a walk. Peckham Rye Park was handy and if we were particularly lucky a band would be playing in the bandstand on the Rye. Or perhaps we would go to Brenchley Gardens, especially if the gardens were full of colour. I have to say that I did not particularly enjoy these outings because I had decent clothes on and I was not allowed to take a ball.

Harold Elven

Collecting for NSPCC

On the right-hand side of Queen's Road going west beyond the RACS store were three successive turnings – King's Grove, Montpelier Road and Carlton Road. At about the age of thirteen I remember canvassing these roads with a friend of the same age for donations to the National Society for the Prevention of Cruelty to Children. We pushed donation envelopes through the house letter boxes one evening and then, an evening or so later, we called to collect them. It was all done after dark on winter evenings but I do not recall either my friend or me having the slightest qualm about our safety. What I particularly remember was the generosity of the donations. Often they seemed to be more than the donors looked as though they could afford. Our collecting efforts were rewarded with tickets for an NSPCC rally at the Central Hall,

Westminster. One of the speakers was the rather lovely Wightman Cup tennis player, Kay Stammers. Seeing her made our evening.

Norman Lenton

My Early Films

At the beginning of the High Street was Peckham Police Station. From a very early age I liked police stations and policemen. They always seemed so reassuring. About a hundred yards on down the same side of the road was the Peckham Gaumont cinema. I saw quite a number of films there but the one that stays in my memory was the 1935 version of *Mutiny on the Bounty* starring Charles Laughton and Clark Gable. The film was classified 'A' so my friend and I were taken by his father. We were too young to see anything other than 'U' films on our own. I did go to the Tower Cinema in Rye Lane. It was the only cinema I have been to with a long flight of steps leading up to its entrance. My recollection is that the films shown at the Tower were either big films that had already been round the major circuits or films that the major circuits did not consider sufficiently attractive. The only film I saw there that stays in my mind is *Give Me a Sailor* (1938). Bob Hope was the star and I believe it was no more than the third film he made.

Norman Lenton

Nunhead in the FA Cup

My understanding was that Nunhead grew from Nunhead Green. The word 'Green' puzzled me when I was very young because the open space that was so called was covered in black asphalt with not a blade of grass to be seen. I used to pass Nunhead cemetery and use the Brockley Footpath that ran alongside it when I walked to One Tree Hill. The cemetery was a dark and forbidding place but with my deep interest in cricket I did once venture into it to find the grave of Bobby Abel (1857-1936), the Surrey cricketer. My main interest in Nunhead was the Nunhead Football Club. It played in the amateur Isthmian League on a ground next to the Haberdashers' Aske's School sports ground. The entrance was in St Asaph Road. My school football team had first call on me on Saturdays but if Millwall FC were not playing at home when I was free I used to watch Nunhead. The highlight of my watching them was when in the 1935/36 football season they survived the qualifying rounds of the FA Cup and on 30 November 1935 played the professional club Watford in the first round proper. They lost by four goals to two but it was a splendid achievement by a team of amateurs to have got that far in the FA Cup. The hero of Nunhead FC was their goalkeeper, Eric Mulley, whose career culminated with an England Amateur International cap. He was also an outstanding wicketkeeper, and later President of Honor Oak Cricket Club.

Norman Lenton

Films at Chepstow Hall

I'm going back to about 1915 when my sister took me to Chepstow Hall in Peckham Road. It was a cinema. The front was a shop that had been left empty. It was taken over by an American. He wore a stetson. As we

Peter Norman and John Smetham enjoyed making model aeroplanes.

walked through the shop door we were given a small bag of sweets. Then I saw a tripod with a square box which had a turning handle. The cinema was opposite the 'Peckham madhouse', as it was called.

Cecil Edgell

The Model Aero Club

The Peckham Model Aero Club flourished briefly at the end of the 1950s having been formed in January 1957. Aeromodelling was a compensation for some of the hardships. For me as a youth, model building and flying represented an escape from the disciplines of school, and from a scarcely-heated Victorian house lit by 40-watt bulbs. The same, or similar, seemed to apply to my friends. To see one's own creation, however rough, taking to the skies in emulation of the birds was heady stuff. Young and old flocked to Ivydale Road School for the first meeting of the club. On one memorable weekend we did fly our model aircraft on Peckham Rye, braving the many curious spectators, the tree in the centre, and various dogs. The favoured venue was Epsom Downs. A pilgrimage to this hallowed ground meant a lengthy ride on a 37 bus to Clapham Junction where we caught a train. Some enthusiasts cycled fifteen miles with a model on their back. The Peckham Model Aero Club continued until 1963.

Peter L. Norman

Wilson's Penny Day

Once a year it would be Wilson's Penny Day. The news soon reached us and all the local children would gather at their field, which was quite near the Rye and Austin's. All the rides on the fairground cost one penny. How the news got round I have never found out but it was a great day. I still chuckle when I think about some of our ideas of a lark – little Londoners growing up in a dodgy world. It was an unhappy hard time for many families. It was colourless. We had to make our own fun.

Kathleen Adams

My Favourite Building

I loved my walk along the noisy Peckham Road with its horses and carts, lorries, buses, trams and an occasional steam lorry, plus the smells. I never ever saw an accident although they did occur, but the traffic would jam up sometimes. In Peckham Road was a large double-fronted shop which was a workshop for blind people. The men worked at machines making knitting needles and others sat weaving beautiful baskets. They were mostly war-blinded men. My favourite building of all time came next, the Camberwell Central Library. It was a low red-brick, very imposing Victorian building. In the evenings and Saturdays the young librarian would patiently try to interest us in books. She encouraged me and my friend Doreen to learn *The Night Before Christmas* for a Christmas show. I was a pain and had to be prompted but Doreen was very good. I can smell those leather-covered books whenever I hear the library referred to today. There were always groups of men crowded around the newspapers, stuck on a board outside the library, looking for 'situations vacant'. It was a sad, grey time for so many people. Behind the building were the library gardens. A little man, with a huge stiff cap almost covering his face, sat in a hut at the entrance and as soon as we approached he bawled, 'No games or running'. What a joyless place it was! It had some unhappy looking bushes and few people were ever there. It was overlooked by The Walmer Castle, the local pub. The Union building which came next was indeed a beautiful building and always cared for. I usually crossed the main road about here to some quaint old houses, Regency and Georgian I think, with intriguing railings and well-worn steps. Then came my

John Barnes prepares to fly his model aeroplane.

school gates. It had a handy sweet shop next door, selling treacle toffee at one penny a quarter.

Kathleen Adams

Wonderful Value

The cinema was our main entertainment as we grew up. The Tower Cinema was the tops and once boasted an orchestra. We also went to the Queen's Hall. This was a little, tatty picture palace not too far from home. It was near where the Odeon was being built about the time I left Peckham. The Tower Annexe was in Rye Lane but I never went there. The Gaumont, which was built in the High Street, was lovely. An afternoon at the pictures cost sixpence for an adult and fourpence for a child. Two pence bought a quarter of sweets. For one shilling my mother and I enjoyed a main picture, the news, a cartoon, a second picture and a variety show with the stars that we heard on our radios – the sand dancers Wilson Keppel and Betty (very popular), acrobats, the big bands, Billy Cotton and sometimes old music hall stars. I remember seeing Albert Whelan and Harry Champion. It was wonderful value and took us far away from the dreary dark days.

Kathleen Adams

The Old Nun's Head at Nunhead Green was replaced by the present pub in 1934. In 1930, when this photograph was taken, the proprietor was Edward Hazel, who is seen here with his wife, Ada, and their son Herbert. Edward Hazel ran the pub for twenty-seven years until he retired in 1933 aged about seventy-eight. He is buried in Nunhead Cemetery.

CHAPTER 8

Churches

This church at the corner of Bellenden Road and Danby Street was opened in 1885 as a Methodist Free Church belonging to the United Methodist Free Churches. In 1907 it became known as Bellenden Road United Methodist Church. It was bought by Hanover Chapel, a Congregational church, in 1920. A Pentecostal congregation purchased it in 1979 and renamed it Faith Chapel.

Air Raid Tragedy

The Unitarian Church in Avondale Road (now Rise), which I attended for several years from the 1920s, seated about 150 people in centre pews and two sides. It had a very fine pipe organ with hand-pumped bellows. It had quite an ornate pulpit of carved wood. The church was lit by gas until electricity was installed. The Revd Magnus Ratter was the minister until he went to India. The church, hall and some houses were bombed in May 1941. My cousin and his baby were killed in the same air raid.

Leonard Moncrieff (Canada)

The Band of Hope

When I was very young I used to go to the Band of Hope which was held in St Mark's

A children's Christmas party was held in the Avondale Road church hall, in Bellenden Road, in December 1938.

church, Harder's Road. I loved it and can still remember singing, 'Where did you come from baby dear?' and 'Little brown seed, O little brown brother – are you awake in the dark?'

Myrtle Newman

I Was a Sunbeam

The Gospel Hall was a real favourite with the children. They kept to simple meetings – more singing than praying. Alternatively we would go to the Salvation Army in Nunhead which was a very happy meeting. I joined the Sunbeams to be able to get a dress and hat. The dress was grey with a bright yellow sunbeam on the hat. I was very upset

when I had to give the hat and dress back, when the novelty of being a Sunbeam wore off. I can look back now and really say I loved and enjoyed my childhood in Peckham.

Marina M. Clayton (née Morris)

Pub became Vicarage

I knew the woman who ran the Eagle pub, Miss Webb, before it became Father Potter's vicarage. I often saw this lively clergyman who wrote two interesting books – *Father Potter of Peckham* and *More Father Potter of Peckham*.

Lilian Burden

Ministry of Love

When I went to Peckham I remember, only too well, the impression made upon me as I did a tour of some of the back streets .... I confess that Peckham made me set my teeth and clench my hands and vow a vow to God that if I did nothing else I would work out a ministry of love for the bairns .... I wanted to reach those whose lives were in a shadow, whose playground was the gutter and whose faces were more frequently tarnished by tears than suffused by smiles.

Revd George Ernest Thorn
Clifton Congregational church, c. 1908

The 'Kissing Church'

My grandmother called Rye Lane Chapel the 'kissing church' because she often passed by when the congregation were gathered on the pavement after shaking hands with the minister; some people kissed each other goodbye.

Leonard Phillips

Alices Smith and Goodall

There was always something going on every evening at Peckham Wesleyan church, Queen's Road, which I attended from being a baby: Brownies, Guides, Boys' Brigade, choir, Young People's Fellowship and Class Meetings. The Sunday School used to collect halfpenny and penny coins to support foreign missions. Two of the most lovely and dedicated Christian women I have ever known were my mother's Sunday School teachers – Alice Smith and Alice Goodall. My parents always attended

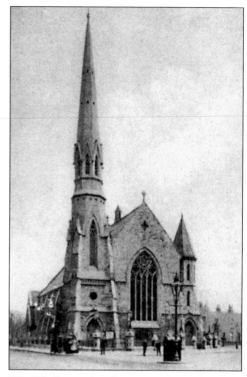

The Wesleyan church in Queen's Road opened in 1865.

Peckham Wesleyan church so I think that's why my middle name is Alice. St Mark's church in Harder's Road had a bell. If it stopped after the second ringing on a Sunday morning, we knew that we were late for our own church.

Lilian Buckley

Parents Rested

Most children were sent to Sunday School with their bible and hymn book as well as a penny for the collection. Parents enjoyed a well-earned rest while the children were away.

Grace Smith-Grogan

The Bun Fight

At the Gordon Road Mission, at the corner of Crewys Road, my sister and I enjoyed helping in the Christian Endeavour for children. They were mostly from deprived homes; some lived in one room. One little girl arrived on a very cold day dressed only in a cotton dress and her mother's shoes.

We decided to invite the children to a party. There were long trestle tables laid out with tasty sandwiches, jellies and home-made cakes mostly provided out of our own money. How they enjoyed it! When they had eaten their fill, a bun fight started. The boys pelted one another with pieces of bun. We tried to start some party games and I had painstakingly made little prizes for them but after their meal they all ran off home. We learnt a lot from that experience. We tried putting on a show for the parents to enjoy. The costumes were made from cast-off clothes, newspapers and coloured crepe paper. Stage curtains were made from old borrowed curtains – all colours, shapes and sizes sewn together. Everyone enjoyed the fun. The children learnt their lines perfectly and sang beautifully. The parents thanked us profusely.

Grace Smith-Grogan

Tabernacle Services

On the first Sunday in May in the 1930s there was a well-attended service at Peckham Rye Tabernacle at 7 or 7.30 in the morning. People attended from various churches. After going to the early morning service I went home for breakfast and then went to my own church, Peckham Park Road Baptist.

Lilian Burden

Rye Lane Chapel

For many years I was a member of Rye Lane Chapel where I enjoyed the wonderful ministry of the Revd Theo Bamber. He was followed by the Revd Emrys Davies, the exuberant Welshman who often startled the rather sedate congregation by bursting into spontaneous song. He had a lovely tenor voice.

Peggy Lovett

First Wedding at Orchard Mission

I first went to the Orchard Mission in 1928, at the age of six, to visit the Cripple Guild of Friendship, attached to The Shaftesbury Society. It was here I first met the boy who would later be my husband! We were both members of this club for many years and I am still in contact with some of the other friends I made there. I was also a Sunday school teacher at the Mission for six years and then we married there in 1944. In 1940 the Mission was opened to receive people who had been bombed out of their homes. A landmine dropped on two roads off Hill Street, which were wiped out. One of the people brought his cockerel into the church with him! They slept on palliasses. When it was really bad we went to the deep shelter. The Superintendent of the church, Donald White, conducted our wedding on 3 June 1944. This was the first wedding to be conducted in Orchard Mission since it was founded in 1887. The entrance to the church was lined with the children from the Sunday school and the Brownies from my pack. The inside was full and I remember the lovely flower arrangements.

Joan Payne

Disruptive in Church

I had one brother who was seven years older than I was, so I could have been quite lonely but I was a gregarious boy and did not lack friends. During the early years I spent a great deal of time at the Edith Road Baptist chapel as my grandmother was a pillar of the chapel and much of my leisure time was based on the activities there. My week at the time, starting on Sunday, was Morning Service, afternoon Sunday school and Evening Service. Monday evening was Lifeboys; Tuesday, Christian Endeavour; Wednesday, choir practice; Thursday or Friday, Bible study. Saturday I spent more often than not travelling around singing solos at various Baptist functions around London as I had, what I now know to be, a rather good soprano voice.

I also remember taking part in many Baptist sporting activities as I loved my sport. Looking back, I realise I was very disruptive in our Bible classes due to boredom – so much so that one year when it came round to be enrolled in the classes, the teacher for my year refused outright to have me in her class! I could imagine the horrified reaction of my parents to this so I begged and pleaded for her to take me on. She relented only on the understanding that I behaved myself and worked. I agreed to this and became a model student. When the results of the scripture exams were published, I discovered I had achieved the highest marks in our chapel and became the recipient of the prized Pesket Memorial Bible, which was given each year in memory of a much revered superintendent. This was an honour which normally went to adults. The reaction from all and sundry was 'You can do it if only you will try'.

Harold Eleven

Church Kept Us Busy

Although I was an Anglican, my friendship with Methodist families led to my attending two Methodist churches. The first was the Methodist church at Kitto Road, New Cross,and the second, the Queen's Road Methodist church. These two churches, together with the New Cross Methodist church, made up a local circuit. The church ministers usually conducted services at all three churches in rotation. At Queen's Road Methodist church I attended Sunday morning and evening services and Sunday school in the afternoon. It was a vibrant church community and gave me the opportunity to take part in a number of extra-mural activities. These included playing table tennis and cricket and appearing in plays put on by the church in the church hall. After evening service on Sundays in the summer a friend and I used to go for long walks. The longest was one June evening when we walked to Croydon Airport. One thing I particularly remember was that at the site of the church, Queen's Road narrowed considerably and outside the church the tramlines ran closer to the kerbstone than anywhere else that I can recall.

Norman Lenton

Worship at St Luke's

The local church which I attended was St Luke's in Rosemary Road. In the early thirties Father Douglas administered to his flock from amid a cloud of acrid incense every Sunday morning, creating a sense of awe but still radiating benevolence.

Stanley Kettel

Proud of Our Uniforms

My sister and I went to Oliver Goldsmith School and I remember well the kindly policeman who used to see us across the road. James Grove Mission, at the Rosemary Road end of East Surrey Grove, played a major part in our young lives. We went to Sunday school there and also joined the 201st company of the Girls' Life Brigade under the direction of Captain Daisy Ashurst, assisted by Lieutenants Smith and Dyson. We were so proud of our uniforms and spent several happy years with the company. Later we joined the youth club. By then James Grove was known as North Peckham Baptist Mission. It was there I met my future husband.

Peggy Lovett

'The Evil of Strong Drink!'

I went to Avondale Road Unitarian Church for Sunday school and Band of Hope from the age of three until I was seven. My sister and I, together with three other children, walked to the Band of Hope in the evening. Sometimes we would enjoy lantern slides. The man in charge would disappear behind the projector draped in a long black cloth which went right over his head. His movements made us giggle.

We witnessed such harrowing scenes of intoxicated men being pulled away from the pub by wives and children, all pale and wearing ragged clothes. Oh the evil of strong drink! There were also the old stories such as *Eric* or *Little by Little* and *He died and never called me mother*. We would always weep real tears at the heart-rending scenes

Girls' Life Brigade members from Rye Lane Chapel and Peckham Rye Mission gathered with others for a special GLB rally at Crystal Palace in 1927.

This baptismal certificate was presented in 1905. The church was badly bombed in the Second World War.

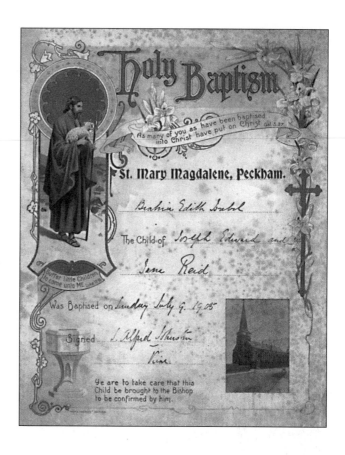

and return home thoroughly upset – or be comforted by buying chips from a small fish and chip shop we passed on the way! We would eat them on the walk home to the horror of my mother who gently chided us by saying, 'Nice children do not eat in the street.' We felt the streets were so dark that nobody would notice – but it just wasn't the thing to do.

Grace Smith-Grogan

Sang the Wrong Words

I was born in Nunhead Grove in 1925. My grandmother, mother, father, brother and I lived in a small terraced house. After I was

married my husband moved in as well, for a while. My schooldays were lovely. I loved school and would not stay away if I could avoid it. I was able to play in the street and go to Peckham Rye Park for a picnic. I remember the first time I went to Sunday school. I told my mother we had sung a song 'Jesus loves us once a week'. It was some time before she discovered what we had actually sung was 'Jesus' little ones are we'.

Doris Daniels

CHAPTER 9

Peckham Rye Common and Park

The bandstand on Peckham Rye was opened on 11 July 1889 by the Earl of Meath, chairman of the Parks and Open Spaces Committee of the London County Council. It was one of a pair designed by Capt. F. Fowke and erected in the Royal Horticultural Society's Garden in Kensington in 1861. The other was moved to Southwark Park. The Peckham one was partially destroyed by a land mine during the Second World War. As it was a danger to children, it was blown up.

Children on the Rye

I was born in 1916 at Tresco Road. With my twin brother and my sister we moved to Waveney Avenue where we lived until 1928. In those days our evenings and free time would be taken up with all kinds of activities on the Rye. There was always so much going on; it

was the centre of our lives. In the summer the bandstand on the Rye was used on Saturdays and by visiting concert parties in the evenings. If we had any pocket money left we used to go. The hard seats were 2d and the deck-chairs in front were 3d. With a kindly man at the gate we children were often allowed to sit at the front for 2d. By the lake in the park stood a drinking fountain with iron cups chained to the side. Our parents used to tell us not to drink the water as it had been poisoned by the Germans. We believed it then.

As children we were given freedom to use the park but were not allowed to enter the arboretum and we always had great respect for the park-keepers. They wore a kind of light brown uniform with a brown trilby hat with a brass London County Council badge on the front. They kept the park immaculate and woe betide any boy or girl who made a nuisance of themselves. People used to take their dogs to the dog pond which was outside the park gate on the side. We used to sail our model boats on the lake at the top of the Rye near the open-air swimming pool.

Charles J.A. Preuveneers

Toy boats

Children sailed toy boats on the Peckham Rye pond despite being forbidden by their parents as the pond was not clean and had broken glass in it. Next to the pond was the open-air swimming pool where I accompanied my sister and father every morning for a refreshing swim before breakfast all summer. A cold shower followed.

Grace Smith-Grogan

And Home by Tram

I was born in Copleston Road in 1928 and later moved to East Dulwich. I can remember being allowed to go to Peckham Rye on a Wednesday night to sit with my friend listening to the band playing on the bandstand. I can also remember the shouts of laughter as we used to paddle in the dog pond. If we were especially good, on a Friday night we could go to the permanent fair not far from the Heaton Arms. While at the fair we could see people feeding the ducks on the pond on the northern part of Peckham

Children enjoyed sailing boats on the Peckham Rye pond. It was filled in during 1953.

This fountain was a gift of Edwin Jones, co-founder of Jones and Higgins. The unveiling ceremony was reported in The Times *on 2 July 1897.*

Band concerts in the ornate bandstand were a popular entertainment on the common.

Norman Lenton walked along Evelina Road to reach Peckham Rye Park.

Rye. When we wanted to go home, we could easily catch a tram because they ran every five to ten minutes.

Joyce Cordwell

Whole Days Outside

The long summer holidays, which always seemed in retrospect to be warm and sunny, were a joy to me because our group of friends were able to go to Peckham Rye Park to play cricket. During the autumn and winter we would play football there. My mother had no qualms about letting me go for the day. She would pack me up jam sandwiches and a bottle of lemonade and not expect me back until the evening, tired and hungry. We would make our way up Nunhead Lane, under the railway bridge, past the shops, which included the pie shop where they sold faggots, pease pudding, potato scallops etc. We hungry boys would stand outside with our noses pressed against the windows and the delicious smells would make us drool. We would walk on past Nunhead Green and further along was the bus garage which I thought was huge at that time. However, we rarely went that way but took what we considered to be a short cut through Solomon's Passage. There was so much grass on the Rye that we had ample space for our games and when we tired of them we would go into the park where there were swings and roundabouts and of course the pond where we would try to spot the goldfish.

Harold Elven

We Walked for Miles

My sister and I loved Peckham Rye Park which was so beautiful in all seasons. We

Many postcards were produced showing various views of the beautiful park. This one was posted in Peckham at 8.30 p.m. on 11 April 1905.

listened to the band, fed the ducks, played on the swings and generally enjoyed ourselves. The crocus walk in Spring will never be forgotten. One Tree Hill was another favourite place to visit. We used to get a 63 bus from Jones & Higgins to Brenchley Gardens and walk through. We always visited the cemetery while there. We walked for miles.

Peggy Lovett

Peacocks in the Park

The nearest park to my home was Telegraph Hill in New Cross but the ground there sloped so much that it was extremely difficult to play cricket or football. In consequence, my friends and I frequently went to Peckham Rye Common to play these games. We always went there

on foot along Evelina Road and Nunhead Lane. Invariably, on Whit Mondays my father, mother, my brother and I took a picnic lunch and spent the day on the common. Much of the time was spent with my father teaching my brother and me the rudiments of cricket and football. During the day we always went into the rather attractive Peckham Rye Park so that my mother could admire the gardens. Another attraction was the peacocks spreading their beautiful wings.

Norman Lenton

Remembering the Peacocks

My mother was born in 1897, three years after the opening of Peckham Rye Park. She spent her childhood in nearby Stuart Road where her mother had a newsagent's shop. Her name was Millicent and one day when walking in the park with her parents she was dawdling behind when the peacocks let out their cry which sounds like MILL. One frightened little girl soon caught up with her parents again. My childhood, in the 1930s, was spent in Catford. One of our favourite Sunday afternoon walks was to Peckham Rye Park. The park still had peacocks then. To this day the cry of peacocks always reminds me of my dear mother.

Mrs Margery Berry (1994)

Died After Preaching

On Peckham Rye soapbox orators sometimes sounded forth on scripture. My grandmother's brother died from pneumonia after catching a chill while standing on a soapbox preaching one cold winter's day.

Grace Smith-Grogan

A Real Treat

When we moved to Rye Hill Park we were lucky because if we wanted to go down and cross the main road we were on Peckham Rye and close to the park. At one of the entrances to the park an Italian ice cream vendor was always there in the summer. I didn't like the wafers but sometimes could afford to buy a $\frac{1}{2}$d cornet with half lemon water ice and half ice cream. This was a real treat. Peckham Rye Park was always

Boating was popular on the Peckham Rye pond.

This postcard shows the lake which looks natural even though it is artificial.

beautiful with flowers as well as grass to play on. The children's play area had swings and roundabouts. There was always someone in charge to keep an eye on the children. Peacocks walked around the park. I enjoyed watching the bowling green being used. I had great times in Peckham Rye Park.

Barbara Kennedy

Cricket on Peckham Rye

For several years before the Second World War, I attended the Peckham Methodist church and was a member of the cricket team. We played on the uneven and somewhat dangerous pitches at Peckham Rye. On one occasion Walter Finch had his spectacles broken when the ball flew off the pitch at an unexpected angle.

Norman Lenton

Games and Sunday Best

Peckham Rye had hordes of people picnicking on it in the summer. Various games, including cricket and football, were played as well as leap frog. People strolled on the Rye and in the Park. Everyone dressed in their best clothes on Sundays and children were instructed not to run but to walk along decorously. It was also frowned upon if housewives put out washing or sewed, embroidered or did unnecessary work on Sundays. A band played in the bandstand on the Rye. Nearby was the pretty little café which we called the Doll's House.

Grace Smith-Grogan

Hymn Singing

We used to go on Sundays to St Mary Magdalene church and after the evening

This postcard sent in 1905 shows donkeys on Peckham Rye.

Whalebone arches were a popular feature in the park. The story of their origin is told in Peckham Rye Park Centenary.

The Victorian bandstand was often used for concerts.

service was over we would walk to Peckham Rye and gather around the bandstand singing hymns. Many sightseers would join in the singing.

Myrtle Newman

In the Park We Behaved

Peckham Rye was our playground but in Peckham Rye Park we behaved. We watched the old men on the bowling green and other people on tennis courts that were well kept and well used.

Marina M. Clayton (née Morris)

Best Park in London

In Peckham Rye Park beautiful peacocks spread their tails and uttered their unearthly cry. Doves cooed in a dovecote. No wonder my father described the park as "the best in London". When he retired he walked around it every morning after breakfast and fed the birds.

Grace Smith-Grogan

This Hurricane fighter was on view in Bournemouth Road and was featured on the front page of the South London Observer on 19 March 1943. It took part in the early days of the Battle of Britain and after that did quite a lot of work over France. During its exhibition it was sponsored by the personnel of Post 37 (Copeland Road) and nearly £2,200 was raised for Wings for Victory to pay for new fighter planes. Most of the schoolchildren in the neighbourhood visited the bomber and had the thrill of sitting in it. The price to inspect it was a 6d stamp.

Prisoners held on Rye

At the age of ninety-eight I still have clear memories of the First World War. I saw a Zeppelin going across the Old Kent Road.

There was an air-raid shelter in the basement of a brewery in Hill Street, between Goldsmith Road and Frankton Road. After raids, boy scouts went around on their bicycles shouting, 'All clear'. I don't remember any bombs falling on Peckham. There were huts on Peckham Rye for prisoners of war. They were mainly Italian. One of the soldiers guarding them told me off for looking at them.

Lilian Burden

Distracted during Zeppelin Raid

My sister, who was born in 1912, remembers a Zeppelin raid when she was attending Adys Road Infants School. The children were all marched into the ground floor main hall and had to sit in a large circle. They were then handed pieces of silky material and had to unravel the fine threads. This was simply to distract them from the air raid.

Grace Smith-Grogan

It Was an Air Raid

I can remember little about the First World War. I had just started school at Wood's Road. Suddenly the bell began to ring and the 'big girls' and 'big boys', as we called them, rushed down to the infants' hall. It was an air raid. The windows were covered outside with sandbags and we were very frightened. We could hear bombs falling. I cannot remember how much damage was done. Another time there was an air raid when a bomb dropped in Linden Grove. It made a big hole in the road but no one was hurt. I can remember when the war was over my mother took us to One Tree Hill where there were great celebrations and fairy lights all over the hill. It was a lovely sight.

Myrtle Newman

Dancing in Street

One of my early memories was in 1918 at the end of the Great War when I saw people dancing and singing on the wide pavement outside Jones & Higgins' store.

Lilian Buckley

Brick Thrown

I was born in Cronin Road in March 1916 a few doors away from where a brick was thrown through a window of the baker's because he was a German. Shortly afterwards a Zeppelin dropped its bombs in Albany Road and a number of people were killed.

Nellie Thornton

New Play Areas

After the Second World War, the whole area was scarred with bombed sites and many buildings were left with brick copings where railings had gone to the war effort. Many houses had Anderson shelters in their gardens. To us children, after the war, the Anderson shelters became our dens and the bombed sites our adventure playgrounds. Most of these pleasures were gradually removed. The shelters were taken away by the local council and prefabs were erected on many bombed sites. These temporary homes were luxurious in comparison with many of our homes. They had fridges and bathrooms. Not all the sites were built on. Warwick Gardens is the site of Azenby Square which was badly devastated in the

A party was held in 1918 in Blakes Road to celebrate peace after the First World War.

war. It was a favourite place of mine to wave to trains.

Norma Francis

Kinsale Road bombed

In 1944 having put out fire bombs in Gowlett Road and Amott Road, my father and I took a neighbour, a Mrs Green who had been injured in the hand, to Dulwich Hospital. The hospital was full of casualties and people were being carried up East Dulwich Grove on stretchers. How many people now realise that the railings around the flats in Peckham Road near the former St Giles' Hospital are ARP stretchers? There was in fact a V1 bomb at the corner of Kinsale Road. I cannot remember the date but I was by this time in the RAF. I

believe it was one Saturday lunchtime because I had just arrived home (a 36-hour pass) and was sitting down to lunch with my mother at our house in Gowlett Road. We heard the sound of an approaching V1 and then suddenly the engine stopped and we knew it was on its way down and was going to be close. We ducked down on the floor and then there was a tremendous explosion and it sounded as if it was in our road. I rushed to the front door which had been blown open and I could see the column of smoke rising behind the house opposite and there was debris falling into the street. I rushed up Gowlett Road into East Dulwich Road and then down to the King's Arms where I could see people hurrying about in confusion. As I reached the corner of Kinsale Road I saw a most terrible scene of carnage and destruction. The air was full of the acrid smoke of the explosion and the dust of the wrecked buildings. The shop on the corner of Kinsale Road had been Coleman's, the florists, and it was now a great heap of rubble with people tearing at the debris to get at people who were trapped. There was the wreck of a double decker bus which had been standing outside. Most of the top deck had been blown away and there were dead and injured in the wreckage. Underneath the bus lay the body of a policeman. I recognised him as a friend of my father's. After the war his name was on a plaque in East Dulwich police station when it was in Crystal Palace Road. I helped with the injured and, as I was holding the hand of a lady waiting to be put in an ambulance, another V1 came over. I remember the fear on her face and how tightly she clutched my hand. Luckily for us that one passed over but no doubt caused death and destruction elsewhere.

There were some amazing escapes. A girl who worked in Coleman's and lived only two doors away from us in Gowlett Road was serving a customer who was killed and Audrey Smalldon was unhurt. The manageress was unhurt but most of her clothing was blown off and I remember a bus driver wrapping his coat around her. I often used to meet her in Rye Lane long after the war had finished. Coleman's moved into East Dulwich Road near Solway Road until their premises were rebuilt. After the Colemans retired, their shop became Glenton Tours.

The Colemans were one of the founder members of Interflora. Austin's had the contract to collect their stocks from Covent Garden Market – even when we had horse wagons. The pubs were open early in the market days. One of our drivers, a Mr Hamilton, had overindulged in the pub one morning. He went to sleep up on the seat of the wagon but the horse knew its way home over London Bridge. Unfortunately, it did not know that it had to stop when a policeman held up his hand and Mr Hamilton was charged with driving a horse and cart while under the influence of drink!

Derek Austin (1995)

Killed in the King's Arms

It was the day following Boxing Day, 1940. I was twenty-one years old and living in my parents' house, 9 Fenwick Road. We were enjoying our evening meal when strange sounds like fireworks swishing down to the ground excited us – swish-whizz-whizz. Some of us rushed into the garden, others to the front of the house. These were incendiary bombs blazing a trail to light up the blackout for the German bombers following along behind. The whole street was filled with people frantically putting the fires out. We then noticed a 'fire bomb' on our roof. My father rushed up five flights of stairs to the top back bedroom (flat roofed). He jumped through the skylight, put the bomb in a pail of earth and carried it spluttering into the garden and buried it. Meanwhile another had fallen down a chimney and was busily burning a settee. At long last all was under control.

We stood warming ourselves in front of a coal fire when suddenly all hell opened up. Bombs came raining down. Suddenly there was a terrific noise. 'This is it,' called my father, 'this is ours'. The house vibrated, shook and trembled and a wall fell down away from us. We scrambled out to the front door to be met by just a gap. We stood in the front garden and looked straight through to the back garden. We thanked God that we were still alive. We faced the back of the King's Arms public house. A landmine had fallen and the parachute had tangled in a tree. It then exploded. The whole area was devastated. King's Arms was practically demolished as were the very large houses in East Dulwich Road. Large blocks of flats fill the space now. The first few houses in Fenwick Road on either side were almost completely demolished. Ours was badly damaged. A coffin was brought out from the house opposite us followed later by another. Two people had been killed in that house. Another few yards and it would have been us. People sheltering in the cellar of the King's Arms were all killed. It is said that on the date that the bomb dropped ghostly voices can still be heard singing the German war song *Lilli Marlene* – a song our soldiers adopted. Kings-on-the-Rye, as it is now called, bears no resemblance to the old building.

Grace Smith-Grogan (1994)

War Declared

Sixty years ago today [3 September 1999] I was in Peckham Methodist church. At the beginning of the morning service the minister said war had been declared. He then pronounced the benediction and sent the congregation home.

Lilian Buckley

Saw the King and Queen

In September 1940 when I was seven our family lived in Copleston Road and I attended Dog Kennel Hill School. One day when I was at school during play time I saw a big car pull up. While I had my arms on the school gate, out got King George V1, Queen Elizabeth and the Queen Mother. The King and Queen Mother walked to the flats where thirty-seven people had been killed the previous night as a bomb scored a direct hit on a crowded street shelter in Albrighton Road. Queen Elizabeth asked me whether my family had been bombed out the previous night. After taking my arms off the gate, I went back one step, curtsied and said, 'No, Madam, I live down the road near Grove Vale School. I am waiting to be evacuated from here.'

Irene Goodwin (née Sherwood)

Dad Came Home

My earliest memory is of being taken to meet my Dad when he came home from the army after the Second World War. I would have been about two and a half years old and Mum took me down Rye Lane towards the bus stop. We reached C&A and Dad was coming towards us. I can remember being picked up in his arms and putting his hat on my head.

Norma Francis

Parents listened to wireless

During the Blitz we spent our evenings and nights in the shelter in the middle of the square at Acorn Buildings. When we were indoors my parents listened to the wireless and my mother knitted or did sewing.

Winifred MacKenzie (née Steel)

The Anderson Shelter

The Blitz altered everything. Areas of Peckham were destroyed by bombs intended for the docks and I can remember children in siren suits scrabbling amongst the rubble in search of treasures. There was a nightly ritual of preparing for the shelter. We had our own Anderson shelter in the back garden and, as darkness fell, we would fill up all the kettles in case the water main was hit during the night and go to the shelter with a box containing important documents, thermos flasks and sandwiches, books and board games to pass the time, although the only lighting we had was from hurricane lamps. The entrance to the shelter had to be carefully blacked out so that no light showed. A familiar sound was that of Air Raid Wardens promenading and shouting, 'Put out that light'. One thing I can vouch for is the spirit of the people – there was never the slightest indication of surrender.

Joan Brown

Spoke to German Prisoners

When the Second World War came, my father joined the Home Guard; ill health prevented him from joining the forces. My mother joined the Women's Voluntary Service and was one of the few women taught to use a gun when it was thought war was imminent. There was great excitement when a barrage balloon was installed in the Sumner Road flats. We children would dare each other to run under it. We had an Anderson shelter in the back garden and a table Morrison shelter in the living room which we shared with neighbours. We were all in it when the property opposite took a direct hit. We were covered in dust and debris. It was a terrifying experience and we were thankful when the 'All clear' went. Usually we children went out looking for shrapnel and compared it with our friends' samples – but not that day! We experienced the doodlebugs which were frightening.

My sister and I were evacuated several times but returned home on occasions when it seemed that the bombing had eased up. We saw much devastation and hardship. When the war was finally over there was a big street party. It was amazing the spread that was put on by the resourceful women during a period of rationing.

I remember the Italian prisoners of war coming. They were billeted in huts on Peckham Rye. They made lovely gardens. Then the German prisoners of war came and a group of us from Rye Lane Chapel used to speak to them. We were amazed to find how very ordinary they were and that they and their families had also suffered. They did not want the war any more than we did. My parents would have been furious if they had known that I had spoken to the Germans.

Peggy Lovett

Church Destroyed

One of the big tragedies in our area was the landmine which destroyed the church in St Mary's Road. The crypt had been a shelter for local people and resulted in many deaths.

Harold Elven

Ernie Fox was in the Lyndhurst Grove Junior School football team in 1938/9 which won the league and cup. He is second from the right on the front row.

Evacuated to Kent

War had been declared! I doubt if we had too much idea of what that meant or was going to mean. During the Munich crisis I can recall playing in the local street with two friends, Bernie Stubbs and John Walton and we cockily dodged imaginary bombs, no sweat! Evacuation was a strange event in as much as the whole enterprise was apparently carried out in complete secrecy. The parents didn't know where their children were going and it seemed almost as if the teachers were acting under sealed orders! We were marched down to Peckham Rye Station, with large luggage labels with our names written on them, tied through our coat buttonholes and carrying our little suitcases and our gasmasks in their little cardboard boxes. The suitcases were probably made of cardboard also. Not much Gucci in Peckham in those days! Eventually, after all the suspense and secrecy, we arrived at our destination which was to be our safe haven from the yet to be experienced Blitz. The destination was Sevenoaks, eighteen miles from Charing Cross and directly under the flight path from northern France to London! At Sevenoaks, probably the Bat and Ball station, although I cannot be sure, we were taken by bus to Godden Green, a hamlet perhaps a mile and a half or so outside Sevenoaks. Yes it did have a village green and a pond with a motley assortment of ducks, muscovies, mallards, geese and the like. It still has to this day a village green and for a couple of miles around appears as if nothing has changed in the sixty intervening years.

There on the village green all the little

The wardens of Post 37 organised this float in about 1943. The Brownie is Doreen Side (now Spence) and the sailor boy was her brother Fred.

evacuees were assembled. I have no recollection of seeing any other boys from our school. The village green was crowded with children and the atmosphere was part 'boot sale' and part cattle auction with a touch of animal refuge. The government had encouraged people to billet the evacuees by offering a maintenance allowance for each child. So ... stroll up! Stroll up! Take your pick while they last. And the kind folk did just that. They strolled up and took their pick. Throughout the afternoon, the chosen, in their ones, twos and threes, went with their new guardians. Many had good experiences and a number kept in contact with their temporary foster parents for long after the war. I still correspond with the daughter of one foster mum, who is an extremely lively and 'with it' octogenarian, the daughter that is!

Ernie Fox (Queensland, Australia)

Father was a Warden

In the Second World War my father was one of the Wardens at Post 37 in Copeland Road. My brother and I attended Peckham Rye School but for three of the war years we were evacuated to Bideford where we had a good time.

Doreen Spence

Returned to Peckham

During the Second World War I travelled to work every day, never knowing how I would get there – bomb craters, blocked roads and railway lines, and I would always end up by walking part of the way. Then tragedy really struck. A land mine was dropped on St Mary's church and the blast made all the

In 1943 Wardens of Post 37 (Copeland Road) gathered outside the Heaton Arms to raise money for War Bonds.

During Wings for Victory Week, Wardens from Post 37 had a display in Rye Lane.

Bernard Thomas Anson, Vera Conway's grandfather, served in Egypt during the First World War. He is seen here with his wife, Alice, and their children Hilda and Bernard.

adjacent property uninhabitable. We were safe in the Anderson shelter which my father and brother had dug in my father's beloved flowerbed but we had to rake the debris off as much furniture as possible and look for alternative accommodation. This was found at the top of Honor Oak Road in Forest Hill. After the war we moved to Forest Hill but I returned to live in Peckham forty years later.

By this time the family had dispersed. My sister, who had been widowed in the first year of the war, returned home with her three children, Mum and Dad and aged Grandfather. All the others had married or died and Auntie Joan was left alone in the big house. So she started looking for something smaller – and on the level! (I had had enough of climbing the hill after a day's

work.) The search was on and eventually I saw an advertisement in the *South London Press* for, 'A bijou Chelsea-type cottage' in Peckham! In Peckham! However, I took the address and although I was Peckham bred and had been a constant visitor to the Tower Cinema and knew the Choumert Road Market – I had no idea that Choumert Square existed. The entrance gates were eventually pointed out to me and having passed through, I could not believe my eyes. Anyway – suffice it to say that I couldn't get back to the owner too quickly and the deal was struck. So, here I am, back in Peckham once again and have now been settled in my Choumert Square nest for nearly twenty years.

Joan Brown

CHAPTER 11

Trips around Peckham

After trams came to Dog Kennel Hill, a horse helped to pull them up the steep gradient.

Horses Pulled Electric Trams

I remember when a horse was attached to the front of electric trams to help them climb the steep Dog Kennel Hill. Electric trams came to East Dulwich in 1906.

Lilian Burden

Crystal Palace on Fire

In 1936 I worked in Moorgate and used the railway from Queen's Road Station. When coming home one evening we could see a huge fire. We wondered where it was. Suddenly a passenger shouted, 'It's the Crystal Palace'. We couldn't believe it, but sadly it was true. When we arrived at Queen's Road Station we could hear and see fire engines coming from all directions. When I arrived home my mother said, 'Come out to the garden and see the sky' – it was a brilliant orange and mother was shocked when I told her it was the Crystal Palace.

We often went from Peckham Rye Station to the Crystal Palace. On the steam

Visitors to the Horniman Museum could take a No. 58 tram from Dog Kennel Hill.

train we would pass our back garden and wave to our mother.

Myrtle Newman

Stole Apples from Nunnery

On occasions when we wanted a change from playing on the Rye, we would pack up all our gear and go to Dulwich Park which was quite a walk up Barry Road. During the spring the park was very beautiful with many rhododendrons in bloom and I shall never forget the time we saw Queen Mary's car driving round very slowly in order that her Majesty could admire the flowers.

One Tree Hill was another of our haunts, not for cricket or football because it was not flat enough but there were plenty of trees despite the name. Nearby, I remember quite

clearly there was a nunnery. I remember this because to my shame I can recall scrumping apples in the grounds. There I was sitting high up on the tree stuffing apples into my shirt when I heard a shout. Looking up I saw this figure in black from head to toe gliding down the path as if she was on wheels. I did not know who was after me and I didn't wait to find out. I slid down the outside of the tree over the wall and away.

Harold Elven

Obscured View

Many years ago on a visit to Peckham I promised to take my wife to a place not far from Peckham where she could see the whole of London. Being Italian, she was very interested and we set forth to One Tree

Hill and climbed up to the beacon basket. We then turned around and I was astonished not to be able to see any of the London I remembered from my youth. It is really amazing how high trees can grow in forty years.

Stanley Kettel

Rolled down slopes

Sometimes we visited the Horniman Museum where the exhibits would interest us for quite some time until we got bored and went to eat our food in the garden – always supposing we had some food left. The Telegraph Hill parks were other favourite spots and were not quite as far as the Rye.

These parks were hilly and lots of fun could be had there rolling down the slopes and many a time I got into trouble because of the wear and tear on my clothes.

There were also trees to be climbed but care had to be taken as I recall a particularly ferocious park keeper and the cry would often be taken up, 'Look out, Parky!' and we would run.

All these jaunts we undertook on foot. Even if we had any money, which was most unlikely, we would not dream of wasting it on fares. Sweets would be a priority on the rare occasion we did have cash. We would be able to buy such delights as 2oz treacle toffee for one halfpenny, which would last some time, or liquorice strips or bootlaces.

Harold Elven

Trams and buses ran to Horniman Museum via Lordship Lane.

CHAPTER 12

The Peckham Society

Campaigners were successful in saving Clifton Crescent.

Peckham – 1970s to 1990s

My King's Grove house was an ugly duckling, terraced house transformed into a detached property by a German bomb. The hole in the terrace was filled by a 1950s small council block and the stick of bombs could be traced across adjacent streets by similar infilling on Montpelier Road, Meeting House Lane and Naylor Road. But King's Grove had been declared the borough's first general improvement area. Landscaping in 1974 and subsequent years made it an attractive place to settle.

Around and about, Southwark Council had caused more devastation than the Blitz by clearing whole swathes of old streets. Comprehensive redevelopment following so-called slum clearance was fashionable throughout Britain in the 1960s. Having seen the baneful social consequences of giant estates, by the 1970s many local authorities

The Peckham Action Group's headquarters in Peckham High Street was a hive of activity.

were preferring to rehabilitate old streets – but not in Southwark. As its name suggests, Meeting House Lane was one of Peckham's oldest streets. A great chunk of it had been demolished and replaced by the Acorn Estate in the 1960s, but much of its Victorian fabric survived. The arcade of shops opposite St John's, itself a replacement of the original bomb-damaged church, included traditional shops such as family butcher, greengrocer, newsagent and suchlike. Today they are a lively Turkish-Cypriot enclave of clubs, dry cleaner and two cafes.

Local pubs accommodated a clientele almost as aged as their interior décor. Folk memories stretched back to the First World War and after, when children played in the street and no one locked front doors. Those

born and bred in the neighbourhood watched with dismay as a terrace of houses on the corner of Goldsmith Road was demolished, supposedly to create land for industrial expansion related to the old pickle factory on Staffordshire Street. It never happened. The pickle factory recently moved away and the site became an accidental wildlife garden. Demolition around Asylum Road was even more extensive. The road took its name from the Licensed Victuallers Asylum, almshouses built in grandiose Georgian style from 1828 onwards. The rest of the street consisted of handsome Victorian villas but this didn't protect them from the bulldozer. The road had been identified as a link road between Ilderton Road and Queen's Road and the whole of the east side from Culmore Road to

Queen's Road was razed to be rebuilt as part of the Brimmington estate.

The pretty semi-detached villas of Culmore Road also disappeared and a start was made on demolishing Clifton Crescent. Built in Regency style from the 1840s, the crescent was Peckham's finest architectural ensemble (apart from the Asylum, which in 1960 became the council's Caroline Gardens old people's residences). An Asylum Road Action Group came into being in 1974 to resist further demolition, and was the origin in the following year of The Peckham Society as the local Civic Trust society for the SE15 district. In the case of Clifton Crescent the Society was successful in gaining emergency listed building status and forcing the council to rebuild the bit it had already knocked down.

Elsewhere, around Peckham, similar schemes were threatening to destroy most of the old village centre. Half of Peckham Hill Street had made way for the Bells Gardens Estate. The beautiful Consort Road linking Peckham and Nunhead was ravaged in its central section, again to provide industrial land. In 1979 the council launched a new town hall project involving clearance of much of the south side of Peckham High Street. No one would claim that the High Street or Rye Lane were beautiful but they had plenty of character and many long established shops. Manze's pie and mash shop on the Peckham Hill Street corner retained its traditional marbled furnishings. The clock tower of the Jones & Higgins department store overlooked the High Street/Rye Lane junction, with the venerable Kentish Drovers public house adjacent. The emporium, whose first floor was reached by a magnificent curving staircase, was the spit-image of Grace Bros – though it had updated itself to the extent of including a remarkably good delicatessen in its food section.

Another excellent deli' lurked underneath the Peckham Rye Station arches. More traditional food was provided by the (still surviving) Kennedy's pie, bacon and sausage shop. An impeccable pork butcher's hid behind the stalls of the Choumert Road market. Sainsbury's existed with its original marble, cut-glass and mahogany furnishing, sadly replaced by a modern store as part of the multi-storey car park redevelopment of Moncrieff Street (in turn replaced by the multi-screen cinema). Marks & Spencer's backed onto the bustling covered market. Co-op branches stretched the length of the Lane, culminating in the great hall and general store at the tip of the Rye. On the other side of the triangle, opposite the White Horse public house, a fish shop had its own tar-blackened smoking sheds at the rear. Beyond, Austin's supplied second-hand furniture to young middle-class immigrants setting up home in the older streets.

Many charitable institutions were also extant. Churches attracted new congregations of evangelical Christians. Long established community organisations such as The Peckham Settlement, founded by the Union of Girls' Schools for Social Service, continued the philanthropic traditions of local Victorian worthies as described by W.H. Blanch in his epic Ye Parish of Camerwell (1875).

A trend against demolition was signalled when the council proposed to knock down the gaunt blocks of the Camberwell Reception Centre on Gordon Road, London's biggest doss house. Local residents successfully protested and the buildings were converted into smart flats. Peckham began to regain a measure of stability after two centuries of growth, decay, wartime destruction and brutal redevelopment. The Aylesham Centre replaced Jones & Higgins but left the landmark clock tower intact. The bus garage built on Thomas Tilling's Bull Yard depot was cleared for a bus turn-around.

Into the 1990s, Canal Head was marked by an entrance canopy. The Peckham Pulse leisure and health centre rose on the long derelict land behind the High Street and the audacious new Peckham library opened in time to salute the new millennium. Most dramatic of all, the vast Camden and North Peckham estates, completed only in the 1970s, were largely demolished and replaced by social housing on a more humane scale.

This writer's great-uncle Horace Smyth and family lived in Talfourd Road behind the Peckham Road fire station in the early half of the last century. As mayor of Camberwell borough 1930/31 he presided over a municipality still strongly Victorian and Edwardian in character. Some of the feeling of the 'Victorian Suburb' described by historian H.J. Dyos survives into the year 2000 more cherished than in the post-war decades of destruction climaxing in the pivotal 1970s.

Bob Smyth, 1999
Peckham Society chairman 1975-78,
Consort ward councillor 1978-83,
Southwark Council deputy leader 1982-83,
Southwark Wildlife Group chairman 1982-85,
author of City Wildspace (1987) and
Forest People and Places (1998)

The Peckham Society

One evening in the Autumn of 1975, a young Bob Smyth called to ask me to join The Peckham Society. It was a month old and Bob was the first chairman and one of the founders. He had discovered me because I had just founded the South West Rye Lane Residents' Association, in response to environmental problems our locality was suffering because of an industrial site in our midst.

Thus began for me an unbroken association for the next twenty-five years with the Society and also continuous education in local environmental matters, local history and community development. In those early days, we had regular monthly meetings in St John's church, Meeting House Lane in the north of Peckham. The formation of the Society had been triggered by the threat to demolish Clifton Crescent, a fine and beautiful Georgian terrace just off Asylum Road. The newly fledged Peckham Society succeeded in having it listed and it has since become the magnificent sight it is today, especially when viewed from the train.

Through Society meetings I learnt about such things as streetscape and traffic management, Southwark's wildlife, Peckham's history and how our predecessors fought successfully to preserve our open spaces like One Tree Hill and Peckham Rye. It was inspiring to feel that we were carrying on that important tradition of active local citizens caring for their history and locality for future generations.

Peckham Action Group

In 1976, I became the secretary of the Society. The Peckham Society had entered my blood! Encouraged by Bob, I delved into the Council's ideas about the future of the centre of Peckham. I was shocked to discover that there were plans for a huge new Town Hall and dual carriageway sweeping right through the area from Southampton Way to Queen's Road. The Peckham centre would be obliterated. At a public meeting in May 1978 (in the Pitt

*Fire-eaters entertain
people in Peckham High
Street.*

Skeletons waited at a bus stop.

Street Settlement, now demolished) local residents and local traders called for opposition to the plans. Thus was born the Peckham Society Action Group, which rapidly metamorphosed into the Peckham Action Group (PAG) as a separate organisation, for which I was pleased to act as Convenor. Over the next four years PAG, with the help especially of Peter Bibby and Nick Snow, worked tirelessly on the campaign and initiated a sister organisation, the Southwark Campaign, which opposed the huge new Town Hall plans. Members of political parties from the Socialist Workers' Party on the left through the spectrum to the Conservative Party on the right, all the local trade unions, as well as numerous individuals, community groups and local traders, stood with each other on marches and demonstrations and public meetings.

Skeletons Waiting for Buses

The Society and PAG worked together closely and I became the Society's Vice-Chair. The Society was able to retain its more sober demeanour, while PAG stimulated widespread publicity with creative activities, including a punk record! One day we had a community festival in the High Street, with fire-eaters, people on stilts and lots of other fun on the (now long gone) triangular traffic island at the junction with Peckham Hill Street. Meanwhile two full-sized skeletons sat at a High Street bus stop holding placards asking, 'Why are we still waiting?' We also took the Council to the High Court for having breached some arcane procedure, and some of us slept in the houses on Summer Avenue for several days trying to prevent their demolition. It all generated extensive national publicity.

Peckham's Centre

The base for the campaign had become the four shops at numbers 2 to 8 Peckham High Street. We had brought these empty shops back into vibrant life. PAG's slogan was, 'Face-lift for Peckham, not a heart transplant', a good expression of the conflicting views of what was needed for the area. Sadly, although we won the battle against the massive plans – they were dropped by the Council in 1980 – the following twenty years produced only a patchy facelift. I watched with sadness over the years as the vegetation took root on the sides and tops of some of the buildings in the High Street.

An important legacy of the PAG campaign was the extension of the 'linear park' into the High Street. The park itself follows the line of the bed of the former Grand Surrey Canal which ended at Canal Head in Peckham. The Canal had been filled in just three years before the Peckham Society was founded. Two traders, Whitten Timber and Abbey Rose, the builders' merchants, had settled and flourished here as their supplies were delivered along the canal. PAG produced alternative ideas for the area including the extension of the park into the High Street. Over the following decade Whitten's relocated to Eagle Wharf itself and Abbey Rose moved near to Consort Road, thus removing the access obstacles to the High Street from the linear park.

White Elephant in Moncrieff Street

Though the plans to demolish the Peckham centre were no more, the Council still wanted to demolish half of Moncrieff Street for a new Sainsbury's multi-storey car park. We knew that this would be a white elephant, because of public reluctance to use such car parks. We went to a public inquiry in 1980 because people were to be evicted from solid good homes they had lived in all their lives to make way for it. We lost the battle but were proved right. Eventually a street level car park was built just a street away from the Aylesham Centre and Safeway store (on the old site of Jones & Higgins). A few years later, the new Sainsbury's closed, replaced by the store less than a mile away on Dog Kennel Hill, in spite of the vigorous OTDOGS (Opposition to Destruction of Open Green Space) campaign.

Police and Community Dialogue

One Saturday in 1981, I was in the PAG shop on the High Street when news started to arrive about disorders on the Brixton streets, two miles away. These events led to the Scarman Inquiry and eventually to the setting up of Police and Community Consultative Groups (PCCG's) to develop good communications between the police and the community. In London there is a PCCG in each borough. In 1987, I became the Peckham Society's representative on the Southwark PCCG (SPCCG). Since then, I became Chair of the SPCCG and an active member of the London PCCG Forum which brings all the London PCCGs together. There is exciting potential for PCCGs in London because they are one of the few, perhaps only, community bodies in a London-wide network, where people of all races, cultures and religions work together in the common good.

Transition

Ron Woollacott took over as Peckham Society chairman in 1977. I well remember the Peckham Society committee meetings on Sunday afternoons in the Woollacott house in Gordon Road. By 1982, many of us felt drained by the previous four years and with the battle over, PAG was suspended, and the Society became mostly dormant. I was delighted however that, at this time, the local energy found its way into the creation of FONC – the Friends of Nunhead Cemetery. Eventually Ron became the long-standing chair of this internationally renowned organisation. In the meantime, Nicholas Reed had moved into Peckham and volunteered to revive The Peckham Society. So the wheels began to turn again and new members were recruited, including Peter Frost, the Society's current chairman.

The Peckham Experiment

I learnt through the Society of the famous Peckham Experiment which took place between 1926 until 1950. Two far-sighted doctors, Innes Pearse and Scott Williamson, led it because they wanted medicine to cultivate health (ethology) rather than just cure sickness (pathology). A pioneering building was designed and built in St Mary's Road to house their Health Centre. I was keen to see if we could bring alive some of the ideas in today's Peckham, so in 1988 held a public meeting in the building, then used as offices, about the lessons from the Experiment.

Although there was significant enthusiasm for the ideas and a Southwark Healthy Cities Network was established, this did not take root at the time. Since then, the Council has initiated a new health centre – the Peckham Pulse – on the site originally destined for the Town Hall and dual carriageway that The Peckham Society defeated. The Peckham Pulse has a number of features inspired by the Peckham Experiment, but sadly there is no acknowledgement of this important local history in the building itself.

The Heart of Peckham

So this area, which would have been covered by a massive Town Hall and dual carriageway, is the site of the new Peckham Town Centre, the Peckham Pulse and the new Peckham library. These developments have been accompanied by the demolition of the Sumner and Camden Estates, to be replaced by houses of the original scale which were demolished to make way for those large estates. Only time will tell whether these new houses, so hastily designed and built to meet central government timetables, escape the fate of the Camden Estate which received awards from all and sundry in the first years of The Peckham Society's existence.

I came to live in Peckham in 1973 because I was attracted by its human scale, at least those parts which had survived the 1960s crazes for demolition and building large estates. After the battles of the late 1970s, Peckham seemed to settle into a slow decline. But this was deceptive. New housing on the empty land brought new people to the area; and people from far off

A man on stilts walks around during a community festival.

lands also settled here. Rye Lane was changing its character, with many exotic food and low cost shops, while Lordship Lane was beginning to provide high quality organic food and specialist shops. None of this was 'planned'. It was the result of natural changes in the life of the local community, forever shifting and changing as the years roll by.

Now the 'planned' major surgery to the north of Peckham High Street has changed the skyline and will also change the social life of the community. Some lessons have been learnt from the past and there is some attention to community participation and for human scale living and working. My favourite local place, with its magnificent trees – the triangle between Peckham Rye and Rye Lane – has managed to survive both the great storm of 1987 and the planning process.

The Peckham Society continues to have an important role to play. The friendships that have developed during its campaigns are not the least important part of its role in the community and these can be life-changing in their own right, as I know from my personal experience. They are a vital part of our civic infrastructure. Long live The Peckham Society!

Eileen Conn, 2000